Phil Fragasso | Craig L. Israelsen

YOUR
NEST EGG
GAME PLAN

HOW TO GET YOUR FINANCES BACK ON TRACK AND CREATE A LIFETIME INCOME STREAM

CAREER
PRESS
Franklin Lakes, NJ

YOUR NEST EGG GAME PLAN
EDITED BY JODI BRANDON
TYPESET BY EILEEN MUNSON
Cover design by The DesignWorks Group
Printed in the U.S.A. by Courier

To order this title, please call toll-free 1-800-CAREER-1 (NJ and Canada: 201-848-0310) to order using VISA or MasterCard, or for further information on books from Career Press.

The Career Press, Inc., 3 Tice Road, PO Box 687,
Franklin Lakes, NJ 07417
www.careerpress.com

Graphics Credits
    "Human Capital"graphic in the Introduction courtesy of Ibbotsen Associates, a Morningstar Company.
    "Safe Initial Withdrawal" graphic in Chapter 3 from Michael Kitces, Kitces Report, May 2008 issue, *www.kitces.com.*

Library of Congress Cataloging-in-Publication Data
Fragasso, Philip M., 1950–
    Your nest egg game plan : how to get your finances back on track and create a lifetime income stream / by Phil Fragasso and
Craig L. Israelsen.
        p. cm.
    Includes index.
    ISBN 978-1-60163-083-4
        1. Retirement income—Planning. 2. Finance, Personal. Israelsen, Craig L. II. Title.

HG179.F69 2010
332.024—dc22

                                                                                2009034265

For our better halves  *who make* *us whole:*
Laura and Tamara.

ACKNOWLEDGMENTS

Every book begins as a vague concept, morphs into a written proposal, and is fully realized when its printed and bound embodiment hits the shelves. And while the authors enjoy the temporary fame and glory that come with having one's name listed in *Books In Print,* many people contribute to the finished product and they need to be recognized and thanked.

Our literary agent, Michael Snell, proved invaluable in helping to hone the content and structure of the book, and the team at Career Press—including Michael Pye, Adam Schwartz, Kirsten Dalley, Diana Ghazzawi, and Jeff Piasky—has been a model of efficiency and support.

Special thanks to Eric Bruyn who created and organized the various charts and graphs and did so with personality and humor. And Craig much appreciates the folks at *Financial Planning* magazine (Marion Asnes, Pam Black, Pat Durner, and Jennifer Liptow) for providing a venue for his research.

And then, of course, we come to our families. Craig is especially grateful to his wife, Tamara, for serving as a pitch-perfect sounding board for his analytical ideas; and Phil thanks his wife, Laura, for her Socratic-like ability to hone ideas down to their core. Our children—Craig's seven and Phil's two—are always present in our hearts and minds; and nothing we accomplish can match the pride of fatherhood.

C ONTENTS

I NTRODUCTION:
Understanding the Cycles of Life and Money

If there's any good that comes from the global economic meltdown of 2007–2009, it will be the long-overdue realization that working-class Americans desperately need help with their investments. In 2008 alone, retirement plan accounts lost more than $2 trillion in value. Participants in 401(k) and other employer-sponsored savings plans stopped contributing and began requesting loans. They were scared and confused, and most of them had nowhere to turn for help. Their retirement dreams were in shambles alongside their 401(k) account balances.

And although the global financial crisis spawned from a wide range of social, economic, and political factors, the increasingly widespread retirement income crisis resulted directly from a conscious sidestep by both the federal government and U.S. corporations. According to the U.S. Government Accountability Office's 2007–2012 Strategic Plan:

Providing retirement income security in the United States has traditionally been a shared responsibility of government, employers, and individual workers. However, the burgeoning federal deficit, especially in federal retirement programs such as Social Security and Medicare, and the declining coverage of employer-provided pension plans suggest a shift in responsibility to individual workers for ensuring an adequate and secure retirement.

Think about it. In our parents' generation, people spent their entire careers with a single company, retired with a lifetime pension, and collected monthly Social Security checks that represented a significant portion of their pre-retirement income. Today's workers face a startlingly different prospect. If you have an employer-sponsored pension plan, you're among the lucky minority of Americans. Traditional defined-benefit plans—in which retirees were guaranteed a specified amount of income for their life and the life of their spouse—are a thing of the past. They have been replaced by defined-contribution plans (most commonly known as 401(k), 403(b), and 457 plans) that shift the burden of building a retirement nest egg that can generate lifetime income from the employer to the employee. And this is happening at a time when that indeterminate "lifetime" will almost certainly be longer than any of us imagined. It's overwhelming, and the vast majority of us are woefully unprepared and ill-equipped to handle the responsibility that has been thrust upon us.

To make matters worse, the process of generating consistent and sustainable income in retirement is characterized by even more trap doors and trade-offs than we face during our wealth-accumulation years. Successful investing requires a systematic plan and the ability to ignore the emotionally wrenching ups and downs of the market. That systematic approach becomes even more critical during the income-producing years of retirement because we have less time and opportunity to make up for mistakes.

The good news is that a workable solution is well within reach of most middle-income Americans. The pivotal first step is to stop thinking about your 401(k) and IRA accounts as an end onto themselves. Rather, view them as the means to the ultimate goal of creating an income stream that lasts a lifetime. At its core, *Your Nest Egg Game Plan* is focused on helping people turn their *individual* savings into *individual* pension plans. And it is indeed all about the "I" in *individual*. There is no one-size-fits-all approach. Each individual's circumstances, needs, and goals are unique. Nonetheless, there are some key attributes that every individual's Nest Egg Game Plan must possess. And that is how we've structured the book. Each chapter focuses on a specific characteristic of a successful investing and income strategy—and to keep things really simple, we've used an *I*-centric approach to emphasize the individuality of each investor's Game Plan. The end result will be an income-generating investment strategy that is Intelligent, Informed, Introspective, Inflationary, Inexpensive, and Inspired.

The I-Stages of Money

Before we get started, let's take a step back to better understand the context of where we came from and where we're going.

Most individual investors and financial advisors fixate on two phases of money management: capital accumulation when we're working and capital preservation when we're retired. And though it's hard to argue with the core of that concept, it's too simplistic to provide any true insight into how our relationship with money evolves over time. A more modern perspective identifies three distinct stages of money management.

Illiquidity	Investable	Income-Producing

The cycle begins with *Illiquidity*—a phase that typically lasts from college graduation into one's 30s. During these early years, individuals may possess nothing but illiquid assets. Their net worth is likely tied up in their homes, 401(k) plans, automobiles, and personal belongings. Being "house poor" or "car poor" is more the norm than the exception. At this stage of life, illiquidity is of little concern because a regular salary covers daily expenses, optimism reigns supreme, and peak-earning years are yet to arrive. In addition, the most important asset of the young worker is his or her intellectual capital—and, although it is impossible to precisely value that asset, it is an individual's intellectual capital that will drive the accumulation of wealth in the later stages of one's career.

Ibbotson Associates, an independent research and financial consulting firm specializing in asset allocation and portfolio construction, has developed a graphical depiction of the interrelationship between human capital (or intellectual capital) and financial capital. The chart shows how our human capital, defined as "an individual's ability to earn and save money," initially represents 100 percent of our "net worth" as we begin our careers. Over time our human capital gradually declines and is supplanted by our ever-increasing financial capital, or saved assets.

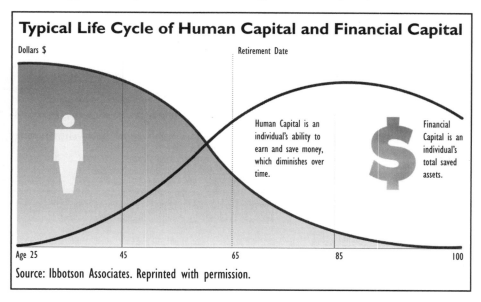

Typical Life Cycle of Human Capital and Financial Capital

Dollars $

Retirement Date

Human Capital is an individual's ability to earn and save money, which diminishes over time.

Financial Capital is an individual's total saved assets.

Age 25   45   65   85   100

Source: Ibbotson Associates. Reprinted with permission.

This graphic is interesting on many levels, but we'd draw your attention to one element in particular. Take a look at the vertical line that bisects the chart, labeled as "Retirement Date." You'll notice that human capital, even at age 65, continues to represent a significant portion of total net worth. There are three reasons for this. The first is the recognition that retirees still have plenty of knowledge, experience, and skills to contribute to the greater good of their families and communities. We don't stop thinking because we stop earning a regular paycheck. The second reason is that our human capital continues to pay dividends in what Ibbotson calls "Deferred Labor Income." Over one's lifetime, human capital converts into financial capital. Part of that conversion process is represented by the salary we earn, and part represents the accruing of lifetime income benefits in the form of Social Security or a traditional pension plan. Ibbotson has calculated the future value of these Social Security and pension payouts and incorporated them into the value ascribed to human capital at age 65. The third reason is that 65 is a totally arbitrary retirement age. Many people choose to continue working full-time or part-time long past age 65 and, whether we choose to do so or not, we have the human capital to further increase our financial capital.

As we move into middle age the focus changes to accumulating *Investable* assets. Retirement still seems far away, but college tuition looms large right around the corner. Disposable income is reaching a high point and a wider variety of investment options need to be considered as one's nest egg reaches the "serious money" level. Diversification becomes paramount, and the two certainties of life—death and taxes—take on a new perspective. This is the stage when lifestyle decisions and investment temperament play a major role in how you manage and juggle your savings and expenses. Temptation is everywhere as the media bombards us with marketing messages trying to separate us from our hard-earned dollars. Whether it's flat-screen televisions, oversized gas-guzzling SUVs, designer coffee, chic apparel that makes last year's chic apparel look like dowdy detritus, or all-inclusive cruises to nowhere, we're forced to make a conscious decision to spend or save. And the decisions we make at age 40 and 50 have a profound impact on how we live in our 60s, 70s, and beyond. These monetary decisions are quite similar to the choices we make in other aspects of our lives. For example, many of us are choosing to eat healthier and exercise more. In effect, we're making a lifestyle decision today that will affect our future well-being. We're making an investment that will pay dividends in improved health several decades down the road. The choice between spending and saving provides the same opportunity. Forgoing the eight-cylinder convertible for a four-cylinder sedan today might mean that, during retirement, you won't have to forgo the occasional four-star restaurant dining experience instead of a nightly four-ounce frozen dinner entrée.

Retirement triggers the third stage of money management, and this is where everything comes together or falls apart. *Illiquid* and *Investable* assets get repositioned into *Income-producing* assets designed to create a steady and reliable substitute for one's working days' salary. The trip wire is that no one knows for certain how long income will need to be produced. What is certain, however, is that many retirees will spend as much time in retirement as they did working, and the lifestyle choices you made in your peak-earning years will inevitably help you or haunt you. And while you cannot undo the financial errors and omissions of youth and middle-age, it is never too late to maximize whatever size nest egg you have and build a game plan to make it last a lifetime.

The 3 Stages of Money and the 3 Boxes of Life

The old adage that "you can't tell a book by its cover" has a lot of application to *Your Nest Egg Game Plan.* At first blush, the book would appear to be all about money—how to earn it, invest it, and make it last.

Such a narrow focus, however, would do a great disservice to our readers and would waste an opportunity to contribute to a truly satisfying retirement experience.

Money certainly plays a major role in retirement planning, but it cannot be allowed to take center stage and deliver a monologue. The well-planned retirement represents an ensemble tour de force with financial concerns sharing equal billing with psychological, emotional, cultural, and physical considerations. In a very real sense, we should be training for retirement the same way an athlete or musician trains to achieve peak performance. When athletes talk about "being in the zone" they refer to much more than the physical ability to hit the game-winning three-pointer; and when musicians interpret Beethoven in a way that brings tears to the audience's eyes, their success goes far beyond their physical interaction with the instrument. Being in the zone is truly a transcendent state in which the musical instrument comes to life and the arc of the basketball's flight takes on a life all its own. And just as dribbling represents "the basics" of basketball and playing the scale constitutes the foundation for a music career, money and investing are the starting points of retirement but not the true endgame. Money cannot buy happiness during our working years, and that is equally true for our retirement years.

Richard Bolles, author of the best-selling *What Color Is Your Parachute?*, wrote a later book entitled *The Three Boxes of Life*. Bolles describes the feeling of being boxed in—of having externally defined walls drawn around most everything we do—and he focuses on what he calls the three "Big Boxes" of life: education, work, and retirement.

Education	Work	Retirement

Instead of viewing life as a continuum, our society tends to fixate on distinct stages of life with very little overlap. As Bolles describes it, "these periods have become more and more isolated from each other. Life in each period seems to be conducted by those in charge without much consciousness of—never mind, preparation for—life in the next period." So there is a clear demarcation between our early years (when we are learning and preparing to become contributing members of society) and our middle years (when we are producing and achieving) and our retirement years (when we presumably stop learning, producing, and achieving and enjoy non-stop leisure). Although this characterization of the three boxes is clearly overstated to make a point, this perspective remains all too common and explains why so many retirees are bored and unhappy in their so-called golden years. As author and inspirational speaker Og Mandino observed in *The Greatest Miracle in the World,* "True security lies not in the things one has, but in the things one can do without." Too many retirees discover that they have not prepared to "do without" work and as a result fail to achieve the "retirement security" they envisioned.

The unhappy retirees never truly prepared for retirement or considered how lifelong learning and achievement would be powerful complements to leisure activities. They never embraced the continuum depicted here.

There's another major difference among and between the three boxes that affects how people approach and either succeed or fail in retirement—the relative level of autonomy. Retirement often represents the very first time that people are responsible for their own day-to-day activities. There are no parents, teachers, bosses, or coworkers to lean on for guidance or blame for our mistakes. We become the parent, teacher, and boss; and we become both the problem and the solution. It can be heady stuff for the unprepared, but there is no excuse for being unprepared. Whether you're already retired, about to retire, or are decades away from retirement, build yourself a holistic Nest Egg Game Plan in which your "nest egg" includes all of the attributes that bring happiness and meaning to yourself and the people around you. A single book cannot pretend to accomplish all of that, but it's our hope to set you on the right path and help you identify your location and direction.

Building Your Nest Egg Game Plan

The best way to think about your Nest Egg Game Plan is as a means to convert your 401(k) and IRA savings into a traditional-style pension plan. To accomplish that you need to start thinking more like a pension fund manager rather than a retired person on a fixed income. To that end, *Your Nest Egg Game Plan* borrows from the approach used by institutional investors, endowments, and large pension plans to help retirees utilize the techniques of true diversification, low-cost indexing, and asset liability matching to construct and monitor a lifetime income stream. Most importantly, *Your Nest Egg Game Plan* does not provide a set-it-and-forget-it framework. Successful investing requires a significant time commitment at every stage of life, and it becomes critically important to diligently monitor your finances during retirement.

Our goal is to provide an easy-to-understand and easy-to-implement framework to design an individualized investment program that will provide the benefits of a traditional pension plan—while offering the flexibility that retirees and pre-retirees demand. Instead of fixating on how much money is saved today or how much money you need to save, focus on how much income will be needed in 10 years, 20 years, and 30 years. And then complete the process by developing a strategy that emphasizes the *reliability* of that lifelong income stream.

We've tried to provide a wide range of insight and tools to build your income-generation plan and conduct annual reviews of your progress against the plan. The knowledge gleaned from the book will also serve as a springboard for in-depth conversations with your financial and legal advisors, as well as your spouse and other loved ones.

None of this is rocket science, and there is no reason that most people cannot successfully implement the Nest Egg Game Plan on their own. However, and this is an important "however," if you feel that you need assistance, do not hesitate to seek out a qualified investment advisor (preferably one who works on a fee basis rather than commissions).

This is your money and your life;

enjoy every penny and

every second of it.

I NDEPENDENT:
Living and Retiring on Your Terms

Independence is defined as "freedom from dependence on or control by another person, organization, or state." Additional meanings refer to being "self-governing," "self-sufficient," and "autonomous." In the aggregate, these definitions get to the heart of what retirement should be all about. At its best, retirement is a time when you're no longer beholden to a boss; your children have left the nest and are living independently; your mortgage is paid off; and your time is your own.

Retirement should be a time of personal, professional, and—most importantly—financial independence. But that freedom comes with a price. It does not happen by itself. It requires careful planning, precise execution, and continuous monitoring. Retirement is not a time for a "woulda, coulda, shoulda" mindset. The poor decisions of youth can often be remedied by the passage of time. Retirement offers no such luxury. There are no second chances. Your time on earth is winding down, so make every minute count.

Each individual's retirement vision is unique—and the road to making that vision a reality is equally unique and totally independent of what others might do or plan to do. A truly independent retirement hinges on each individual embracing responsibility for his or her retirement—planning it, managing it, and living it. If you're like most people, you've longed your whole life for independence. And as with most things, you need to be careful what you wish for. *Your Nest Egg Game Plan* was created to help ensure that retirement wishes come true.

The Changing Face of Retirement

Whole forests have been destroyed to support the vast array of books and articles that have been written about the new rules of retirement. Norman Rockwell–style images of idyllic retirements have been captioned with the catchall phrase "this is not your father's retirement." And it increasingly looks like retirement is the next competitive playing field for the aging baby boomers—who can retire first, who can retire richer, and who can cram more diverse and obscure activities into every hour of retirement.

There are many preconceived notions about what retirement should look like depending on where you live, your pre-retirement profession, your interests and avocations, your financial situation, your friends and family, and a slew of other factors. This can create pressure and anxiety not terribly dissimilar to the "keeping up with the Joneses" mindset that afflicts many of us during our working days. Retirement is a time to put this kind of nonsense behind you (if not sooner!). Forget about doing "what's expected" and focus on doing what feels right to you. The homogeneity of the workplace does not have to extend into retirement. Your focus is no longer on accomplishing a corporate goal that was thrust upon you. Your only goals are the ones you set. You are no longer defined by what you do but rather by who you are.

"I'm retired" is a statement that you should never voice or believe. Instead, if people ask, tell them that you've stopped working for the ABC Company but are now training for a 100-mile bike ride, re-landscaping your property, volunteering at the local library, re-reading all the classics you skimmed in high school English, learning to paint with watercolor, re-falling in love with your spouse, or any of several thousand other responses that reflect your individual priorities and approach to life at that point in time.

We don't need to kill any additional trees to make the point that "this is not your father's retirement," just as it isn't your neighbor's, colleague's, best friend's, cousin's, brothers-in-law, or anyone else's retirement. It's yours and yours alone. That's the true "new rule of retirement," and it's a rule you must adhere to vigorously.

Independent but Not Unilateral

Money—earning it, spending it, and bequeathing it—is the most frequently argued about topic among spouses, children, siblings, and other family members. For many people, this issue is exacerbated in retirement because money tends to be in shorter supply and difficult decisions can no longer be put off indefinitely. And in the case of married couples, the abundance of free time and additional time spent together can cause previously repressed financial and interpersonal issues to explode to the surface. For example:

▷ One spouse can't wait to stop working while the other finds value and personal satisfaction in the workplace.

▷ One wants to move closer to the grandchildren while the other wants to stay put or move elsewhere.

▷ One views retirement as a time of rest but the other sees it as an opportunity for adventure and making up for lost time.

> ▷ One has strong charitable and philanthropic aspirations while the other wants to spend to the end and leave what's left to the kids.

> ▷ One wants to plan and budget every step of their retirement while the other wants to play it by ear.

> ▷ One wants to relive the carefree days of youth with a two-door convertible while the other wants a minivan to better entertain the grandkids.

All of these examples support the accuracy of a 2007 research study by Fidelity Investments that points to lack of communication as the primary culprit for couples' differing views of money and retirement. Most glaringly, Fidelity found that 1/3 of husband-and-wife couples disagreed when asked at what age they would retire and the lifestyle they expected to lead in retirement. Another 41 percent couldn't agree on whether one or both of them planned to continue working in retirement. And 58 percent of couples gave differing answers as to whom their spouse would turn to for financial guidance in the event of their death. Not surprisingly, the 23 percent of couples who reported working together and discussing their immediate and long-term financial needs were considerably more optimistic about and better prepared for their retirement. On the flipside, couples who didn't work together on their financial plan were far more uncertain about the future and lacked such basic planning elements as a will.

Retirement may well be the very first time that couples spend extended time together on their own. As a result, one or both of them may feel pressure to do everything together and may begin to feel that they are losing their individuality. In a very real sense, it's similar to the changes a young couple experiences when they first get married and move in together. A lot of compromises have to be made, expectations need to be shared and modified, and two lives need to be blended in a way that still allows for private time and personal space. Waiting until retirement to discuss and resolve these kinds of issues is a recipe for disaster. Address the challenges and potential minefields of retirement long before they become critical.

It's also important to recognize that there is a whole other set of issues for couples who do not retire on the same time schedule. When only one of the partners stops working, the day-to-day relationship between the two will change dramatically. The partner who has stopped working may expect the other partner's full attention when he or she returns home from work. Conversely, the working partner may expect the retired spouse to pick up more household chores and may resent it when that does not happen. There are literally dozens of issues like this that can be addressed and resolved through a candid dialogue.

The key point is that you have to start early. In a recent study, a full 22 percent of retirees hadn't given any serious thought to retirement until six months before they left their jobs, and another 22 percent began serious consideration one year beforehand. Only 28 percent gave their retirement situation serious consideration for more than two years. And when you add up the number of hours most people devote to retirement planning, it's dwarfed by the amount of time they spend watching *American Idol* and similar television "reality" shows, playing fantasy football, and discussing the social lives of celebrities and celebrity wannabes.

Remember how we defined independent as "self-governing" at the beginning of this chapter? If left on its own, your retirement will indeed be self-governing, but you will not be the self who's driving the bus.

The Stages of Retirement

There are a variety of life stages during one's working years: the carefree days of being single, the bliss of young marriage, the joy of parenthood, and so on. The same is true of retirement, and your Nest Egg Game Plan needs to acknowledge and reflect that. Most people, however, build their retirement income plan on the assumption that each year will look pretty much like every other. As a result, they base their lifetime retirement income requirements on how much money they expect to need in their first year of retirement and extrapolate from there. People who do this, and people who subscribe to any of the one-size-fits-all solutions bandied about by television pundits and the popular press, will likely under-spend needlessly in the first years of retirement and/or find themselves in dire straits in their later years.

The problem derives from the common notion of viewing retirement as an event rather than a process and a series of distinct life stages. Robert Atchley, a professor of gerontology at Miami University (Ohio), has written extensively and insightfully on the subject and has identified six transitional phases of retirement. And though no one individual is likely to experience all six phases, Atchley's framework provides a springboard to better understand the different emotions, issues, and concerns we face as we wend our way through retirement.

- ◗ **Phase One: Pre-Retirement:** Although this stage technically spans decades, in reality it begins a few years before retirement and involves gradual disengagement from the workplace and serious thought (or casual day-dreaming) about what retirement might look and feel like.

- ◗ **Phase Two: Retirement:** For most people, this is the "event" part of the retirement process. Just as marriage begins with a ceremony, one's official retirement is usually marked by a going-away party, farewell lunches with colleagues, and joke gifts in lieu of the formerly traditional gold watch. This is the moment when you stop going to the workplace and paychecks cease. For most retirees this ceremonial event leads to one of three paths:

  1. The "honeymoon" path, like its marital counterpart, represents a blissful fantasy of limitless energy and free time. It's an extended vacation with no certain end-point, though it is certain to end.

2. The "new routine" path is followed by people who already lead full and active lives outside the workplace and who simply glide into a fully functioning retirement life style.

3. The "rest and relaxation" path is often followed by individuals who are leaving high-pressure jobs that afforded limited time for personal pursuits. This path provides a buffer zone and allows the new retiree to take a deep breath before defining his or her own retirement routine.

▶ **Phase Three: Disenchantment:** At the risk of belaboring the marriage analogy, this is the phase where the emotional high of the honeymoon dissipates and the retiree misses elements of his former working life and starts to recognize the flaws and deficiencies in his new life. This phase can be exacerbated by other disruptive changes to the retiree's life such as illness, the death of a spouse, or relocating to a new setting.

▶ **Phase Four: Reorientation:** At some point during the honeymoon and disenchantment stages, the retiree realizes he's in retirement for good and, consciously or subconsciously, conducts a self-inventory, considers his retirement experience to date, and paints a broad-brush vision of how he'd like to live out the remainder of his life. This is when people are most likely to get more involved in the community and focus on hobbies and other joyful avocations. It would not be an overstatement to suggest that this period presents a rare opportunity to reinvent yourself with few external constraints.

▶ **Phase Five: Routine:** The term *routine* has become unfairly associated with dullness. A more appropriate association would be with words like *comfortable, familiar,* and *personally satisfying.* The most rewarding retirements are built around a collection of activities and interpersonal relationships that are as comfortable and timelessly stylish as an old pair of jeans.

▶ **Phase Six: Termination of Retirement:** Although death represents the ultimate termination of retirement, increasing numbers of people are experiencing another stage, sometimes quite prolonged, of lost independence due to injury or illness. The routine that they had enjoyed is now gone. Instead of being viewed as and living like retired people, these individuals live out their lives as disabled senior citizens under the care of family, assisted-living centers, or nursing homes. Improvements in healthcare serve to extend this interim period between life and death, and a healthy debate could be waged on the personal and societal pros and cons of extraordinary life-prolonging medical care.

Understanding the various phases of retirement will help you build a more targeted Nest Egg Game Plan and be able to navigate the uncharted waters of retirement with greater confidence and fewer surprises.

The Stages of Retirement Spending and Income Needs

People spend more money on the weekend than on weekdays, and they spend more money when on vacation than when working. So it shouldn't be a surprise that many retirees experience a significant uptick in spending during the first few years of retirement. With the workplace behind them, their new lives represent an unending succession of Saturdays and vacation time that needs to be filled with activity. In addition, the new retiree often has a lot of pent-up demand for long-dreamed-about trips abroad, far-flung educational programs like archeological digs or African safaris, boats or RVs, country club memberships, and the like. For some people, this increased spending can last several years and represent far more than the standard 4 to 5 percent recommended annual withdrawal rate.

This burst of activity and spending makes sense on many levels. Many new retirees experience a "let's do it while we're young enough and healthy enough to enjoy it" attitude. And although some might interpret that approach as a selfish focus on immediate gratification, it

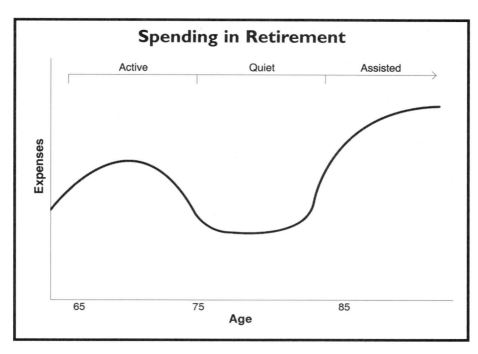

can also be viewed as a realistic perspective and appreciation for the nuances and changing tides of a long-term retirement.

Most gerontologists identify three distinct spending periods in retirement:

▷ The first period, which we've already described, is variously known as the go-go or active years. As you build your Nest Egg Game Plan, you may want to put aside a specific sum of money, over and above your targeted withdrawal rate, to finance this heightened spending without short-changing your later years.

▷ The middle period is a time of quieter and more contemplative pursuits—visiting the grandchildren, taking courses at the local community college, and volunteering. This is often the time when downsizing happens, and retirees sell their home and move into a smaller condo or retirement community. For many retirees, this is the longest lasting period of retirement and, from a financial standpoint, that's good news because it's also the time when spending is at its lowest.

▷   The third stage of retirement spending is characterized by increasing health-related expenses. Coinciding with Atchley's sixth phase, elder retirees often suffer from physical and cognitive impairments requiring multiple medications, frequent doctor visits, and some type of assistance to handle day-to-day living requirements. Out-of-pocket costs for healthcare skyrocket during this period; and even folks who have been diligent about managing their retirement income portfolio may find themselves in a precarious financial situation as they are forced to spend down their assets at a worrisome and unsustainable pace.

There is no simple recommendation on how best to prepare for and handle these differing income needs and spending patterns as you progress through retirement. Managing income flow in retirement is a high-wire balancing act. You don't want to be so frugal in the early years that you don't get to enjoy the freedom of retirement, but you also don't want to dig yourself into a deep financial hole that you can never escape from.

Most importantly, you have to account for healthcare costs. This is where most folks drop the ball because they significantly overestimate the coverage provided by Medicare. Since 2002, Fidelity Investments has been researching the impact of healthcare costs on retirement. The most recent Fidelity study, released in March 2009, states that a 65-year-old couple will pay about $240,000 for healthcare services over the course of their retirement (17 years for men and 20 years for women). That represents a 50-percent increase over the 2002 estimate, reflecting a healthcare system whose costs are rising far faster and more dramatically than the inflation rate for other parts of the U.S. economy. As bad as the $240,000 number sounds, the reality is worse because the Fidelity study does not include the costs of long-term care or dental, vision, and hearing services. Healthcare reform has been a frequent refrain among U.S. politicians, but, until it's a reality, you need to recognize the scope of the financial need as you periodically review your Nest Egg Game Plan.

A Changing Plan for a Changing You

The only universal recommendation we can make is to stay flexible and closely monitor your spending. You need to expect the unexpected, be willing to change your assumptions, and never say never. Decisions that may have appeared unthinkable during the first years of retirement—like downsizing, relocating, taking in a boarder, investing in a fixed annuity, or generating income from a reverse mortgage—may become necessary courses of action later in life.

Just as your income needs change throughout retirement, so do your personal interests and preferences. Think about the difference in your outlook between the ages of 40 and 60. Why wouldn't you expect a similar change between ages 60 and 70, and between ages 70 and 80? The game plan you developed at age 65 may seem laughable 10 or 15 years later. The important thing is to have a plan and to remember the words of Italian writer Giuseppe Tomasi di Lampedusa: "If you want things to stay as they are, things will have to change."

Chapter 2

INNUMERABLE:
Moving Beyond "The Number"

People obsess over "the number." Dozens of books and articles have been written with the misguided intent of helping people determine their one true number—that is, the minimum size nest egg—that will deliver financial freedom and retirement bliss. But just as no two human beings, including identical twins, share the exact same biologic DNA, everyone's "fiscal DNA" is also different. Focusing on a single number provides a superficial answer to a question that everyone asks but that no one truly understands.

So why the obsession with a concrete number? It's due in large part to the mindset of the financial professionals deemed qualified to make such awe-inspiring calculations. Financial planners, accountants, tax attorneys, and actuaries are paid to deliver hard-and-fast numbers. In addition, if you'll allow us to wear our cynical hat for a moment, being able to point to a specific number makes it easier for financial services companies to inflate an individual's needs, scare him or her to the point of paralysis, and sell more product. (See "Is Your Number Too High?" on page 42.)

This idea of an absolute number grew from the traditional belief that retirees would need to replace 80 percent of their pre-retirement income to be comfortable. It's one of those general guidelines that everyone knows, but it is so simplistic as to be meaningless. It ignores such key considerations as: Will the mortgage will be paid off? Are young children or elderly parents still in the picture? Is the retiree a homebody or world traveler? If married, what is the age spread between the partners? What is the retiree's investment temperament and appetite for risk versus guarantees?

Unless You're a Number There Is No Number

The beauty with numbers is that they are absolute. They have a very specific, unchanging meaning. Life, however, is nothing like that. Our lives are meandering journeys that continue into and through retirement. So just as the beliefs we held so dear as young adults—for example, don't trust anyone over the age of 30—seem naïve today, the number that sounds right five or 10 years before retirement may not inspire confidence on the first day of retirement and may seem positively ludicrous five or 10 years into retirement. The presumption that you can project your financial needs for a retirement than could span 30 or 40 years is preposterous. Think about it this way: There's not a corporation in the world that can accurately plan for more than two or three years down the road. What's so different about you and your retirement that makes the planning process so precise?

It's also ironic that so many of us go through life complaining about the dehumanizing aspects of modern-day society that make us feel more like a number than a sentient being. But as much as we don't want to be treated like a number, we want to have a retirement number that we can call our own. Equally disconcerting is the fact that money should never be the determining factor in establishing or ensuring one's happiness—whether during our working or retirement years. This strident focus on an absolute number disavows all the other attributes of a happy and giving lifestyle. Sure, money is important, but some of the happiest people we know have very little money. They're happy because they live rich lives that enrich the people around them. That leads to the most important number in anyone's life: the number of people who are better off because you are a part of their lives.

If despite all our arguments to the contrary, you feel you must have a retirement number, then go with it, but don't obsess over it. Any number you arrive at needs to be monitored, reviewed, and recalculated on an annual basis—because the only number that really matters is the number that works for us at any given point in time.

The Innumerable Problems With Target-Date Funds

The financial services industry is never at a loss for new products, and the hottest new product of the last ten years is the "target-date" fund. These funds carry specific dates in their name—for example, the ABC Investment Company 2015 Fund. The date is supposed to reflect the year when you will retire, and the fund is supposed to become more conservative (that is, have less exposure to stocks and more exposure to fixed income) as the target date approaches.

What's supposed to happen, however, doesn't always come to pass. When Ibbotson Associates, an independent financial services research firm, released its analysis of the 2008 performance of target-date funds the results were not pretty. And though it is not surprising that the funds did poorly in the horrific 2008 market, what Ibbotson found troubling was the extent of their poor performance and the unusually wide disparity of returns.

Consider this. Of the 31 target-date funds designed for people retiring in 2010, the average return was -23.3 percent, but the range of returns varied from -3.6 percent to -41.3 percent. And that dispersion of returns points out the key problem with target-date funds—in other words, what's under the hood?

Target-date funds use a "fund-of-funds" structure to build a diversified portfolio, and the portfolio manager modifies the mix of funds to become more conservative as the target date approaches. In reality, every fund company has its own idea of how to define aggressive and conservative, as well as how and when to evolve to a more conservative allocation. You don't need to read the prospectus to know that the 2010 target-date fund that returned -3.6 percent was heavily weighted toward fixed-income, while the fund that lost -41.3 percent must have had a huge equity position.

This lack of transparency requires target date fund investors to make sure they understand exactly what they're investing in, because the fund companies won't make it easy. Every fund that has 2010, 2020, or 2030 in the name does not follow the same asset allocation approach. That fact is compounded by the realization that not everyone who plans to retire in 2020 has the same needs or risk tolerance level.

The dramatic differences in the performance of 2010 target date funds make them problematic for older people. At the other end of the spectrum, target date funds are generally a good approach for young investors because most 25-year-olds are in the same boat. Their needs are quite similar. They are trying to find a career and, if they're ahead of the curve, they may have a few hundred dollars already tucked away in a 401(k) or an IRA. The makeup of an "appropriate" investment portfolio for 25-year-olds is pretty standard: mostly equities. Virtually all 25-year-olds should have a portfolio that is heavily invested in stocks. Time is on their side and, as a result, the volatility of a stock-heavy portfolio is not a big concern. The uniform nature of 25-year-olds makes it easy for the investment industry to create investment products that meet their needs. In short, 25-year-olds can be effectively and accurately aggregated in terms of their investment needs.

The investment need of 65-year-olds is a very different matter. Generic investment products that were perfectly appropriate for 25-year-olds may not be suitable for a 65-year-old with very specific financial needs and life circumstances. By the time we've reached retirement age our lives have become complex in a vast number of ways. Financially speaking, a 65-year-old is a complex creature in comparison to a 25-year-old single-cell amoeba. Understandably, the financial industry has a much more difficult time serving the needs of retirees with boilerplate investment products like target date funds.

And Please Do Not Rely on the Internet

If you need further proof that there is no simple number, then try calculating your number on a few of the four billion retirement calculators available on the Internet. If it truly were as simple as adding A + B and dividing by C, then you'd expect every calculator to deliver the same solution given the same inputs. But they don't, and to demonstrate that the authors took a test drive on a variety of calculators and are unsurprisingly dismayed to share the results.

Our test subject was a 55-year-old woman earning $75,000 per year. She planned to retire at age 66 and hoped to receive 60 percent of her pre-retirement income ($45,000 in today's dollars). She expected to live until age 95. She had $150,000 in savings and would continue to save 8 percent of her salary until she retired. She expected to earn 7 percent annually on her investments prior to retirement and 5 percent afterward, and she projected an inflation rate of 3 percent.

What we found most interesting was the fact that many calculators didn't ask for or include Social Security in the inputs or output. Now we're just as jaded about the future of Social Security as most of our countrymen, but this omission is outrageous and can only be attributed to the desire to inflate both the need and the shortfall. This first output exemplifies the kind of nonsensical calculations you're likely to find. Cutting to the chase, our test subject was informed that she would need to have saved $1.8 million by the day she retired. Based on her current savings and projected growth, however, she would have a shortfall of $1.5 million. The good news is that the geniuses behind this calculator have a solution: Our test subject simply has to save 98 percent of her salary each year and she'll be right on target.

Cost of Retirement

How Much Will Your Retirement Cost?

Examine these results carefully. As you can see, there is a lot of information to consider. The numbers may look large, but don't be overwhelmed.

The annual income that you will need in your first year of retirement will be:	$69,275
When you begin retirement, you will need to have the following amount saved:	$1,797,926
Assuming no additional contributions, your current savings will grow to:	$315,728
This means that, without additional saving, you will have a shortfall of:	$1,482,198
Each year, you will need to save the following percentage of your salary:	98.00%
In the first year, this works out to:	$73,500

And then we came across this startling analysis which, also totally ignored Social Security and never asked about other potential sources of retirement income such as a pension or rental property. We hope you share our concern that our test subject will run out of money after only 5.3 years.

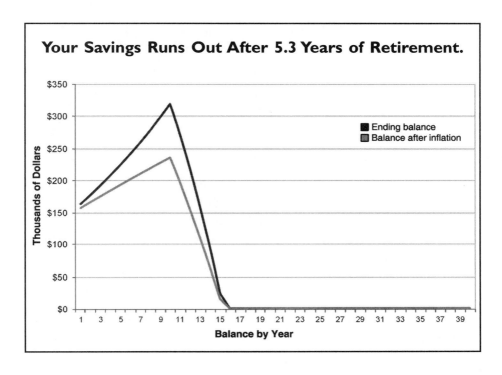

It's hard to choose a favorite among all these analyses, but the chart on page 40 would have to be in strong contention for the top spot. Although it does include Social Security, the chart only illustrates savings and expenses; and the whole thing flat-lines at age 76. Savings and expenses both disappear at the same moment. But that's not the best part. Read the fine print at the bottom of the chart. That's where our test subject was given several recommendations on how to enhance her retirement savings plan, including this gem: "Increase your rate of return before retirement to 18.58%." The scary thing is that the company behind this calculation is not some sleazy web site owner; it's a big, well-known and highly respected firm.

Not surprisingly, some calculators provide you with more than just fear and uncertainty; they're also eager to provide a solution. The purveyor of the following information shown on page 41 informed our test subject that she would run out of money at age 87 but provided no data to back up that conclusion. Instead, it was quick to point out that she "did not have Medicare supplemental insurance" (perhaps because she was only 55 years old), she should consider long-term care insurance, and she might want to consider an annuity as an inflation fighter.

You May Need to Save More.

Your plan provides $358,798 when you retire. This retirement savings may run out at age 76. This is based on retirement expenditures of $64,049 per year. This amount is 60.00% of your last year's income of $106, 748. This plan includes $27,460 per year from Social Security.

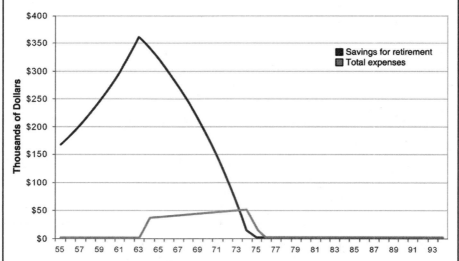

To help meet your goal, you may wish to do one of the following:

▸ Increase contributions to 51.58% of your income ($38,685.00 annual savings, which will increase as your salary increases).
▸ Increase your rate of return before retirement to 18.58%.
▸ Reduce your required income at retirement to 40% of your final year's income.
▸ Delay your retirement until age 84.

Do You Have Enough Assets and Are They Protected?

Inflation, fluctuations in the financial markets, and asset allocation issues can reduce the value of your assets and negatively impact your retirement plan.

You do not have Medicare supplemental insurance. Rising medical costs and an increasing need for medical treatments that are not completely covered by Medicare could quickly consume your assets.

▸ Consider: Medicare supplemental insurance

You do not have long-term care insurance. If you encounter a serious medical problem, your assets could be quickly consumed by the costs of long term care. Long term care is not covered by Medicare nor most supplemental Medicare programs.

▸ Consider: A long-term care insurance policy

Congratulations on owning a home. This asset can help you in retirement. Consider increasing your income with a reverse mortgage, decreasing expenses by refinancing your mortgage, or downsizing to possibly eliminate your mortgage altogether.

▸ Consider: A reverse mortgage

▸ Consider: Refinancing your mortgage

▸ Consider: Relocation

You have significant assets—much higher than average—and could benefit from the counsel of a financial advisor on how best to protect and allocate those monies.

▸ Consider: A professional financial advisor

Inflation can have a devastating effect on your retirement. Depending on the inflation rate, $5,000 today may only buy $2,500 in goods and services in 20 years. It is important to protect your assets from inflation. Annuities with inflation protection and some inflation-proof investments can help protect your buying power.

▸ Consider: Purchasing an annuity

The World Wide Web is a wonderful source of information and entertainment, but remember its limitations. Every byte of information was placed there for a reason, and the reason is not always innocent and pure. *Caveat emptor.*

Is Your Number Too High?

As difficult as it is to find a financial newspaper, magazine, or Website that doesn't opine regularly about the historically low U.S. savings rate, there is a sizeable and vocal group of academics and economists who argue that many Americans are being scared into saving far more than they will ever need. Led by Larry Kotlikoff, a Boston University economics professor and co-author of *Spend 'Til the End: The Revolutionary Guide to Raising Your Living Standard— Today and When You Retire,* this counterinsurgency points a finger at the financial services industry for its self-interested misrepresentation of retirement needs. It all starts with the magical income replacement ratio of 75–85 percent espoused by most financial planners, mutual fund companies, brokerage houses, and insurance companies. Indeed, when we conducted our own test of online retirement calculators, we found that 80 percent was the most common default value for income replacement.

It doesn't take a lot of analysis to see the fallacy of this 80 percent number, because no one—and that truly means *no one*—lives on 80 percent of their pre-retirement income. Keep in mind that the definition of pre-retirement income is your total income and investment earnings. That means it's before federal income taxes (15–35 percent), before state income taxes (0–10 percent), before Social Security (6.2 percent), and before Medicare (1.45 percent) taxes. At the very least, then, the least-taxed of us net a maximum of 77.35 percent of our pre-retirement income, and most of us net something closer to 65%. And remember this is before taking into account 401(k) contributions and other savings, which should account for another 5 to 10 percent of pre-retirement income.

And is there an American among us who hasn't paid for our children's orthodontic work, summer camps, music lessons, and after-school activities? How many of us have paid all or part of our children's college tuition? Don't our mortgage payments represent our biggest expense year after year, and, if we've planned properly, shouldn't they disappear at or shortly after retirement? How much do we spend on commuting to and from work, and buying overpriced lunches and coffees when we're at work or on the road? And do we really need a new car every four or five years or, if we really tried, couldn't we keep a car for 10 or 12 years and save money on both the car payments and insurance premiums? If you follow this line of questioning and start adding up all the expenses that will go away or be reduced in retirement, you can make a convincing argument that most of us could live comfortably on 40 percent to 50 percent of pre-retirement income. And though it's true that some expenses may increase in retirement, most notably healthcare expenses (notwithstanding the cost-efficiency of Medicare), it would be difficult to imagine the replacement ratio creeping up anywhere close to 80 percent.

We say all this with some trepidation because we do not want you to let down your guard and start thinking you can glide into retirement. A successful retirement absolutely requires careful planning and ongoing attention. But it does no one any good to operate out of fear because you know you can never approach an income stream of 80 percent of pre-retirement income. In all likelihood, you won't need to replace 80 percent of your working income, but figure it out for yourself to be sure.

A Case in Point

The very notion of a "number" runs counter to the diversity of experiences and expectations that distinguish each of our lives. As a case in point, consider two soon-to-be-retired couples—the Browns and the Smiths—who seem to have a lot in common including "the number." Here's what they share:

> ⊳   Each husband is 65 years old.

> ⊳   Each wife is 62 years old.

> ⊳   Each couple's pre-retirement income is $100,000.

> ⊳   Each couple has $400,000 in savings and owns a home worth $500,000.

> ⊳   Each husband is eligible to receive $20,000 in annual Social Security benefits.

> ⊳   Each wife is eligible to receive $15,000 in annual Social Security benefits.

> ⊳   Each couple has the same expectations about inflation, performance returns, and longevity.

Based on this information and the 80-percent rule of thumb, you could extrapolate that each couple would need $80,000 per year in income. As they were eligible to receive $35,000 in annual Social Security benefits, they would need to self-fund the remaining $45,000 annual requirement. Using a 4-percent withdrawal rate, "the number" required to generate $45,000 of income would be slightly north of $1.1 million—almost three times the actual savings of $400,000. Looks like these golden years will be heavily tarnished—or maybe not. Let's take a closer look at their respective situations.

The Browns have been preparing for their retirement over the last few years. They have been consistent and diligent savers, contributing the maximum amount to their 401(k) plans ($8,000 per year for each of them), and becoming increasingly conservative as they approached their retirement date. They used Mrs. Brown's final paycheck to pay off their home mortgage, eliminating a $2,000 monthly bill, and they have no other debt. Their federal income tax rate, after deductions, equaled 20 percent. They paid another 7.65 percent for Social Security and Medicare, and 5 percent in state income tax. When you add up all of that, you have total expenses of $72,650—meaning that the Browns would need only $37,350 in tax-free income to replicate their pre-retirement lifestyle. With their Social Security benefits covering $35,000 of that need, the Browns' number is arguably less than $100,000.

The Smiths are a whole different story. Despite their sizeable pre-retirement income, they have been living paycheck to paycheck. They closed out their 401(k) accounts several years earlier and used the proceeds to pay for their children's college tuition. Their $400,000 in savings represents what's left of a $700,000 inheritance Mr. Smith received a few years ago. He invested heavily in U.S. and international equity mutual funds and lost more than a third of the total during the market meltdown of 2008. The Smiths still have $100,000 left to pay on their home mortgage and have another $50,000 of debt on a home equity credit line. The monthly payments on the two home loans equal $3,000, or $36,000 per year. The property tax on their home adds another $4,000 annual expense. They also have outstanding loans on two automobiles totaling $700 a month and monthly credit card bills of $1,000 for "incidentals." To top it off, they pay about $5,000 a year in country club dues. Added up, these fixed expenses total more than $65,000 *without* accounting for essentials like food, utilities, gas, and insurance. Based on this the Smiths would be hard-pressed to live comfortably on 80 percent of their pre-retirement income precisely because they were living far beyond their means during their working years. Unless the Smiths choose to delay retirement, downsize their home to pay off their debt, give up the country club membership, and share a used car, their number will be significantly above $1 million and will be, for all practical purposes, unattainable.

When you take a step back and closely examine your post-retirement income needs, you'll see that your pre-retirement income is a meaningless barometer. Spending patterns are a far better predictor of need than income. In addition, *needs* constitute a far better measure than *wants*. So as you build out your Nest Egg Game Plan, focus on what you truly need—not to the point of asceticism but rather to create a balanced life and a sustainable lifestyle.

Chapter 3

I NEXHAUSTIBLE:
Ensuring You Don't Outlast Your Money

Now that we have diminished if not totally eliminated your obsession with "the number," we're going to introduce the real number that will determine the success or failure of your Nest Egg Game Plan. At the risk of paralyzing you with fear and dread, it would not be an exaggeration to state that determining this number is the single most important decision facing new retirees. In addition, when left on their own, this is where retirees tend to make their biggest mistake.

The number to which we're referring—may we have a drum roll, please—is the amount of money you can withdraw annually from your savings without running out during your lifetime. Most financial professionals counsel their clients to plan on a 3-percent to 5-percent initial withdrawal rate with an annual cost-of-living adjustment to reflect current inflation levels. Most individual investors are far more optimistic and grossly over-estimate how much they can withdraw annually from their savings. In 2008, MetLife conducted a survey of working Americans between the ages of 56 and 65 and within five years of their intended retirement age. Close to half of the respondents—43 percent to be exact—believed they could safely withdraw 10 percent or more of their savings every year. Granted the survey was conducted before the stock market collapsed in the second half of 2008, but a double-digit withdrawal rate seems shocking nonetheless. And although it would be easy to dismiss the issue as another sign of investor ignorance, the financial services industry has to share the blame. Individuals have had it pounded into their heads that the stock market is the best place to invest. Mutual fund and insurance companies trumpet the fact that the annualized stock market gain over the last century equaled 8 percent, 10 percent, or 12 percent, depending on the index and who was doing the calculations. That information then provides the wobbly foundation for most investors' mistaken belief that you can safely withdraw a percentage of your savings equal to the percentage increase in the overall portfolio. In other words, if the market is up 10 percent you can safely withdraw 10 percent. It seems like grade-school math, but it fails in real life because markets do not move in straight lines. Even if the stock market were to deliver a 10-percent average annualized return over the next 30 years, there would be some years with double-digit losses and many years with modest returns in the –5 percent to +5 percent range. Annual withdrawals of 10 percent during down years or slightly positive years would reduce your portfolio to frightening levels at a frightening pace.

So what is the optimal withdrawal rate? The answer is borrowed from Abe Lincoln who, when asked how long a man's legs should be, responded, "long enough to reach the ground." To wit, the optimal withdrawal rate should be low enough to last a lifetime. And that's the quandary. The good news is you're probably going to live far longer than you ever imagined. That's also the bad news. The same MetLife study referenced previously found that 60 percent of the respondents underestimated their life expectancy, and, once again, they are not to blame. We've all grown up reading or hearing about the annually up-dated life expectancy data from the National Center for Health Statistics (NCHS). The latest NCHS data states that a newborn baby boy can expect to live to age 74, and a baby girl can expect to live to age 80. Although interesting, this information has zero relevance to the retiree. Life expectancy at birth assumes that 1/2 of the baby boys born on the same day will die before age 74 and 1/2 will live beyond age 74. By the time someone arrives at retirement age, he or she needs to consult a life expectancy table like the one that follows (provided by the Social Security Administration).

Male-Female Life Expectancy vs. Age

	60	65	70	75	80	85	90	95
Male	20.36	16.67	13.27	10.24	7.62	5.45	3.80	2.68
Female	23.53	19.50	15.72	12.29	9.22	6.62	4.60	3.22

Based on this information, the average 60-year-old man can expect to live to age 80 (i.e., 60 + 20.36 years). Similarly, a 70-year-old woman has an even chance of living to age 85. Most people find this information surprising, which is why they fail to account for a prolonged life when developing their retirement strategy. Ignoring this information, however, makes it far more likely that you'll deplete your assets too quickly.

The 30-Year Plan

At first blush, knowing exactly how long your retirement income stream needed to last would appear to make all the uncertainty about sustainable withdrawal rates irrelevant. In reality, that is not the case.

Michael Kitces, a highly credentialed educator on financial topics and author of the monthly "Kitces Report," offers a unique perspective of historic return streams. Kitces bases his analysis on an all-U.S. portfolio consisting of 60-percent equity and 40-percent bonds, rebalanced annually back to that allocation. Beginning from 1871, Kitces created a graph that shows what percentage could have been safely withdrawn in the first year, adjusted annually for inflation, and fully depleted the portfolio at the end of the 30th year.

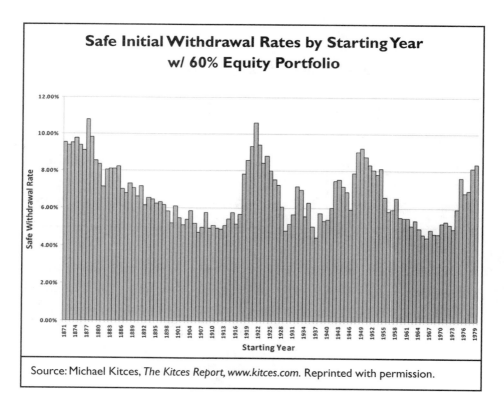

Source: Michael Kitces, *The Kitces Report,* www.kitces.com. Reprinted with permission.

Interpreting the meaning of this graph constitutes one of those glass-half-empty or glass-half-full dichotomies. The half-full crowd would focus on the fact that an 8 percent or higher withdrawal rate would have worked perfectly for one in 10 retiring generations; a 6 percent or higher withdrawal rate worked about half the time; and, in all but a tiny number of years, 5 percent would also have worked out well. Financial professionals, on the other hand, tend to be worriers, and their half-empty reaction to the chart would be that it wholeheartedly supports their recommendation of an initial withdrawal rate of 3–5 percent. The reasoning is that a financial plan needs to be foolproof and able to withstand worst-case scenarios. Hoping you can safely withdraw 10 percent a year because someone who retired in 1922 was able to do so represents a breach of fiduciary responsibility—even if you make that decision yourself.

Another thought-provoking and sobering interpretation of the chart involves its trend line. Although it's not a perfectly shaped sine wave with evenly spaced high and low points, the wave pattern is unmistakable. The safe withdrawal rate rises for several years, peaks, and then begins a steady decline. Looking closely at the six rightmost columns, you'll see a major spike upward in 1974, followed by an even more dramatic rise in 1975. The gains were moderated in 1976 and 1977 and then peaked at a withdrawal rate in excess of 8 percent in 1978 and 1979. Because of the hugely powerful bull market of the 1980s and 1990s, it's a safe assumption that anyone who retired in the early 1980s also experienced sustainable withdrawal rates in the 6-percent to 8-percent range. A few of them might have even approached 10 percent. But like all the other waves in the chart, the upward trend that began in 1974 will also be reversed. Because we know that 2000–2008 was a horrid time for the stock market, we also know that people who retired somewhere in the mid-1990s and later are facing a markedly different withdrawal experience. The two decades' worth of perennial double-digit gains have been replaced by two severe bear markets occurring just six years apart. So check back with Kitces in 15 or 20 years, and you'll likely see that we've made another roundtrip back down to a safe withdrawal rate of 3 percent to 5 percent. You can bet your retirement on it.

3 Critical Variables

The success or failure of your retirement income strategy hinges on the interdependencies of three distinct variables: your initial withdrawal rate, the inflation rate of your withdrawals (that is, the annual cost of living adjustment), and the sequence of returns in your retirement portfolio. The first two variables are obvious and self-explanatory. The third, sequence of returns, is a bit more complicated. As we discussed earlier in this chapter, the average rate of return is meaningless for an income-generating portfolio. Instead, it is the sequence of annual returns that determines how long your money will last. If you begin your retirement in a bear market with two or three down years in a row, you may never be able to recover from the deficit. On the other hand, if you start off with a raging bull market of double-digit gains over several years, you could probably boost your withdrawal rate and still never run out of money. In reality, you can point to four critical success variables—with luck being the fourth consideration.

We've put together a variety of charts that compare and contrast various withdrawal rates, inflation rates, and return sequences. For the purpose of uniformity, all of the supporting data is based on a typical retirement portfolio of 50 percent stocks (represented by the S&P 500) and 50 percent bonds (represented by the Lehman Brothers Intermediate Government Bond index). Later in the book, we'll recommend a more diversified portfolio, but for the sake of simplicity we'll limit the examples to these two asset classes. All of the examples represent a starting value of $500,000 in total retirement savings. From that total, an amount equal to two years' worth of withdrawals is deposited in a money market or other cash-equivalent savings account. For example, using a 4-percent withdrawal rate and a 4-percent inflation rate, the investment account would begin with $459,328 and the cash account would start with $40,672. (Note: The "extra" $672 in the cash account reflects the 4-percent inflation adjustment for the second year.) In addition, rather than using a straight-line compounding rate or randomly generated annual return numbers, we're illustrating 39 years of actual performance from 1970 through 2008. We are purposely excluding Social Security or other types of guaranteed pension payments and are assuming that the withdrawal rate represents what the individual needs over and above Social Security to live comfortably.

Withdrawal Rate

So let's start with what we've already described as the single most important decision you'll make as a retiree: your withdrawal rate. These first three graphs compare what would have happened to our sample portfolio using three different withdrawal rates: 4 percent, 6 percent, and 8 percent. All three charts assume a 4-percent inflation rate applied to the annual withdrawal amount. (COLA = cost of living adjustment)

This first illustration represents every retiree's dream. You get to live comfortably without worrying about your finances, and you get to leave a fortune (in this case, about $5 million) to your heirs or charity.

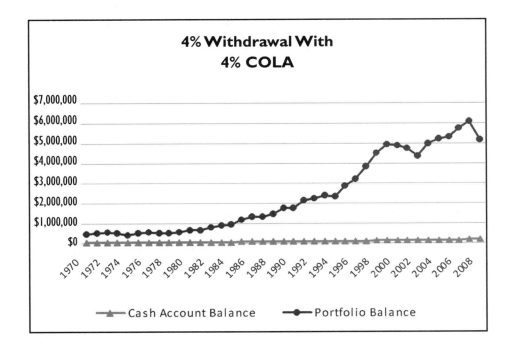

Now see what happens when we bump up the initial withdrawal rate to 6 percent. It's quite a different story. We muddled along for the first decade and then experienced the euphoria of the 1982–1999 bull market. The picture changed dramatically with the bear market of 2000–2002, and our account value fell off the proverbial cliff. Our investment account was totally depleted by the end of 2008—but we still had two years' worth of income in the cash account. In this scenario, the retirement income plan lasted for 41 years so, unless you retired at an exceptionally young age, you still had money in your pocket when you passed away.

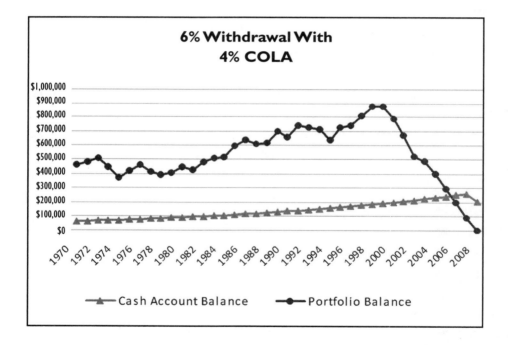

And then we come to the 8-percent withdrawal rate. Keep in mind that 43 percent of respondents in the MetLife survey believed they could safely withdraw 10 percent or more from their retirement account. In this graph we see that the investment account runs out after 16 years and (as in all the examples) the cash account provides two additional years of income. Assuming you retired at age 65, this scenario only supports you to your early 80s and would pose an unacceptable risk to most people.

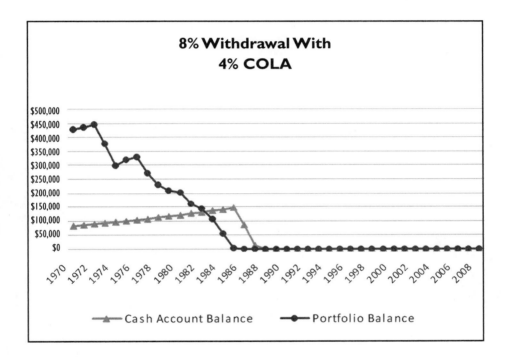

Inflation Rate

Inflation is a true killer to people living on a fixed income, but most folks underestimate its long-term impact on their purchasing power and standard of living. In addition, because the United States has been in a low-inflation environment for the last two decades, inflation is often viewed as a distant threat or a nuisance that can be readily dealt with and alleviated by federal monetary policy. Because of that, many retirement calculators and many financial advisors use 3 percent as a default value when considering inflation. We believe that 3-percent inflation is an unrealistic assumption, especially in light of the huge federal stimulus programs initiated to halt our potential slide into a depression. Though hyper-inflation is not a certainty, we have substantial budgetary deficits to overcome; and it is far more likely than not that we will see a significant increase in inflation over the next decade or two.

Our first chart is a repeat, and illustrates a 4-percent withdrawal rate with 4-percent annual cost-of-living adjustments. All is well.

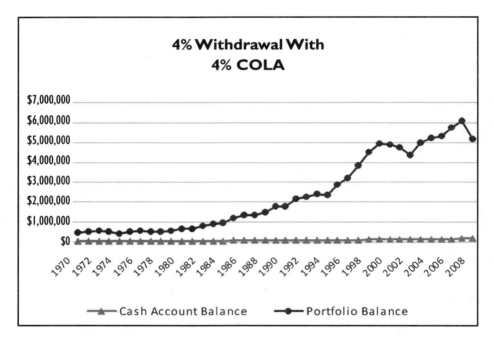

When we increase the inflation rate to 6 percent, and adjust annual withdrawal amounts by a 6-percent cost-of-living adjustment (COLA), the portfolio remains at comfortable levels and has an ending balance of more than $2 million.

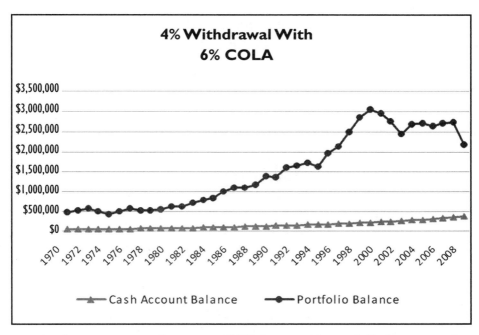

An increase to an 8-percent COLA rate substantially increases the stress on the portfolio, and savings are depleted at the end of the 34th year.

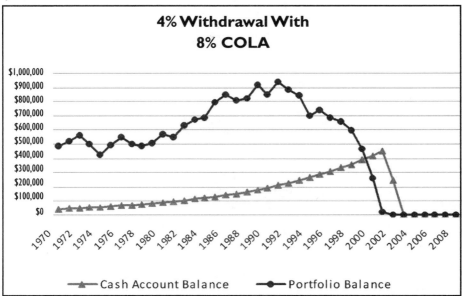

The following graphic illustrates how the portfolio would have performed using cost-of-living adjustments equal to the actual changes in the Consumer Price Index over the period. You can see that the trend line and ending value are very similar to the 6-percent COLA example.

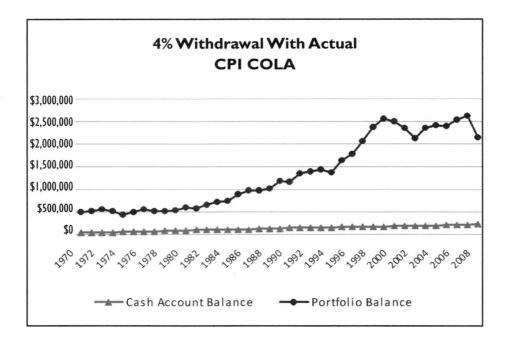

The next chart shows the interaction between the withdrawal rate and the inflation rate. Refer back to the chart showing a 6-percent withdrawal rate and a 4-percent inflation rate. In that scenario the portfolio lasted for 41 years. However, if we change the inflation assumption to use actual CPI data, the result is strikingly different. In this example, the investment portfolio and cash account are totally depleted after just 20 years.

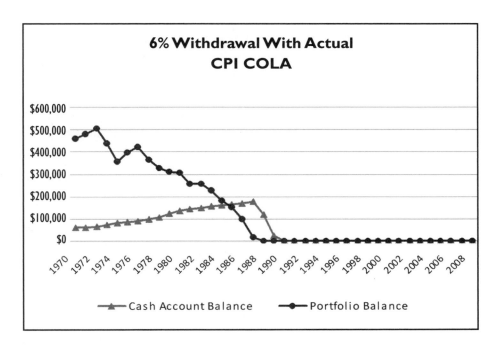

Sequence of Returns

Up to now we've been using actual performance for the 39-year period from 1970 through 2008. When considering the impact of a portfolio's sequence of returns, the performance in the early years has an outsized impact on the long-term success of the income-generation strategy. As you can see from the following table, the 1970s began with three straight years of positive stock market returns including especially high returns in 1971 and 1972.

	1970	1971	1972	1973	1974
S&P 500	3.92	14.30	19.00	-14.69	-26.47
Bonds	16.86	8.72	5.16	3.36	7.03

The strong stock market performance was complemented by unusually high returns in the bond market, including a 16.86-percent return in 1970. The last two years in this time period, 1973 and 1974, were very weak for the stock market and about average for the bond market. And although 1973 and 1974 eroded the portfolio, they were doing so off a very strong foundation so the impact was muted. Taking another look at the 4-percent withdrawal example, using actual CPI data, you can see that the portfolio ended with a balance of more than $2 million.

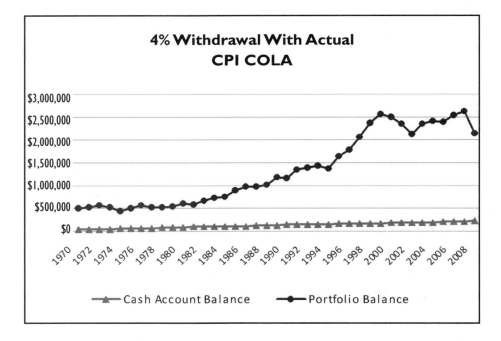

What happens, however, if you start off your retirement with a bear market? To test this scenario we again used the actual performance data from 1970 through 2008, but this time we reversed the sequence so that 2008 represented the first year and 1970 represented the last. The following table reminds us just how horrible 2008 was for the U.S. stock market with a loss of 37 percent.

	2008	2007	2006	2005	2004
S&P 500	-37.00	5.49	15.79	4.91	10.88
Bonds	10.43	8.47	3.84	1.68	2.33

Intermediate government bonds performed quite well in 2008, with a 10.43-percent return, and both stocks and bonds delivered average returns from 2007 to 2004. Nonetheless, the first year's drop in the stock market proved an impossible setback to overcome. In this scenario, the account was depleted after 26 years.

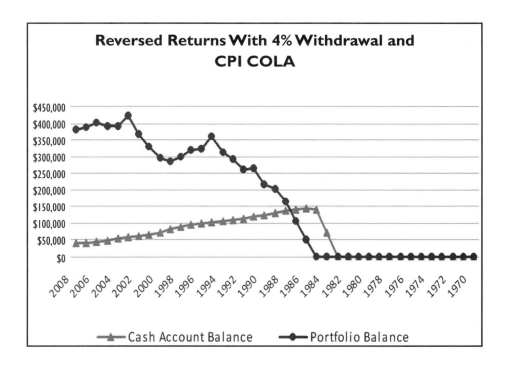

If we increase the initial withdrawal rate to 6 percent, the scenario becomes a train wreck and the portfolio is depleted in just 14 years. If this represented the actual scenario of a healthy woman who retired at age 62, she would find herself penniless at the age of 76 with a life expectancy of 12 more years.

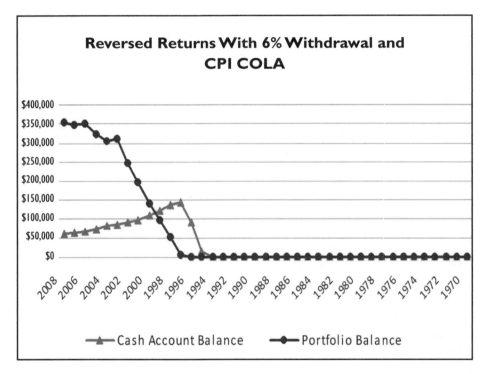

Reversed Returns With 6% Withdrawal and CPI COLA

The Luck Factor

American author Bret Harte tells us, "The only sure thing about luck is that it will change." The same can be said about the financial markets. There is no sure thing in investing or in generating lifetime income. The best you can do is plan for bad luck and, if Lady Luck chooses to smile your way, welcome her with open arms. Planning on good luck to guide your retirement—as many people did in 1999 and early 2000—is a one-way ticket back to the working world.

The Difference Between *Want* and *Need*

The difference between an income-generation plan that is truly inexhaustible and one that is quickly exhausted is often the difference between what we want and what we need. Far too many people live beyond their means during their working years. Indeed that may be why there's so much focus on the need to replace 80 percent of pre-retirement income. If people are living a lifestyle equivalent to 120 percent or more of their working income, then perhaps a target of 80 percent (which would represent a 33-percent reduction from pre-retirement spending patterns) is appropriate. For most people, however, targeting a post-retirement income stream of 80 percent of pre-retirement income is unnecessarily ambitious and creates undue levels of anxiety.

As we state numerous times in this book, retirement is not a specific moment in time. Rather, it's part of our life journey and is built upon and reflective of a lifetime's worth of experiences. If our working lives were characterized by the immediate gratification of credit cards, the prestige of adorning ourselves with Dolce & Gabbana and driving expensive German automobiles (that we lease because we can't afford to own them), and the thrill of being the first on our block to own the latest cool gadget, we're unlikely to magically and dramatically change our behavior just because we're no longer collecting a regular paycheck. Or if we do, we may be forever angry and resentful (though for what and to whom is not clear).

The most effective way to never run out of money is to be terrified of ever running out of money. (*Terrified* is probably too melodramatic a word, but it serves to make the point.) Take the focus off of your *desired* withdrawal rate (which would support an unrealistic lifestyle) and work to define a *sustainable* withdrawal rate that can deliver everything you need and some of what you want. Some people may consider that a compromise; we believe it's the retirement jackpot.

So as you live your life both before and during retirement, consider the wisdom of Og Mandino and recognize that "true security lies not in the things one has, but in the things one can do without."

Chapter 4

I NEXPENSIVE:
Keeping Costs Down to Keep Returns Up

In *The Little Book of Common Sense Investing,* John Bogle, founder and retired CEO of the Vanguard family of mutual funds, tells us that, when it comes to investing, "performance comes and goes, but costs go on forever." He's alluding to the fact that the single most effective way to increase investment returns before and during retirement is to keep your investment-related expenses as low as possible. It sounds easy and it is, but most people ignore it—either out of ignorance or complacency. That's a big mistake, but there are some simple ways to monitor and manage investment expenses.

First off, you need to understand exactly what you're paying for and the relative value you receive for that payment. In general, you incur four types of investment-related expenses:

1. **Transaction fees:** These are typically paid to a brokerage for buying or selling stocks or bonds. There is no way around these fees, so

the key is to find the best combination of price, service, and breadth of product. This is an example of when the lowest-cost provider may not necessarily be the best choice. If you're a do-it-yourselfer, try to stick with a well-known company like Charles Schwab or Fidelity, or check out Barron's annual survey of brokerage firms. If you work with an investment advisor, financial planner, or broker, make sure you understand any and all transaction fees at the beginning of the relationship. And make sure to read the fine print.

2. **Money management fees:** These are charged by investment companies that manage portfolios of stocks, bonds, and other financial instruments. The most common examples are mutual fund portfolios, but money management fees are also incurred within exchange-traded funds, separate accounts, limited partnerships, unit investment trusts, annuities, and just about any product that can fluctuate in value and price. Once again, these fees cannot be avoided but they should be managed, because they can vary dramatically from reasonable and appropriate to truly outrageous. For example, a low-cost index fund might cost 10 basis points (that is, 0.1 percent) annually. An actively managed fund in a niche asset class like emerging market debt or a narrow sector like solar energy might cost 150 to 250 basis points annually; and a hedge fund pursuing arcane strategies will typically charge 200 basis points annually plus 20 percent of all profits. Paying attention to these fees can pay big dividends in terms of increased performance.

3. **Advisory fees:** If you invest on your own, you'll avoid this type of fee, which is charged by some financial advisors. But please, never invest on your own simply to save on advisory fees. You should only invest on your own if you have the knowledge, confidence, and stomach to handle the vagaries of the market without a guiding hand. If you do work with an advisor, understand how he or she is paid. The traditional form of compensation is via commissions. The broker recommends a stock or mutual fund, and he or

she receives a commission on the sale. Though there is nothing intrinsically wrong with this approach, it does open the door to possible conflicts of interest (for example, selling proprietary products or recommending products that pay a higher commission). The other form of advisor compensation is the fee-based approach. In this case the advisor may charge an hourly fee for reviewing a portfolio and making one-time recommendations or may charge an annual asset fee (typically equal to 1 percent of total portfolio value). In the latter example, the asset-based fee should decrease as assets increase. Whereas a 1-percent fee is fair for an account of $200,000, it would be usurious for a multi-million-dollar account. If your advisor charges an asset fee, make sure you're not also incurring high transaction fees, management fees, or commissions because it can add up quickly. A 1-percent asset fee combined with a 2-percent management fee atop a separate transaction fee can put a serious dent in your long-term returns.

4. **Taxation on interest, dividends, and capital gains:** If you're really going to be smart about investing, then you have to consider taxes as a manageable expense. If you're in a high tax bracket, then tax-free investments like municipal bonds could be a good choice—but be sure they are not subject to the AMT (alternative minimum tax); otherwise you'll lose all or part of the tax-free benefit. There are also many mutual funds that advertise themselves as being "tax-managed." That means the portfolio manager tries to offset gains with losses to keep distributions to a minimum. Although this approach may provide some benefit, it's more of a marketing gimmick than a true strategy. The three best ways to manage taxation during retirement is by understanding how different types of investment income and profits are taxed, which investments to own in which accounts, and where to make withdrawals first. The two primary taxation rates are "ordinary income" and "long-term capital gains." The former can run as high as 35

percent, whereas the latter is fixed at 15 percent. Interest payments from savings accounts, CDs, and bonds are considered ordinary income. Most dividend income, however, is taxed at the 15-percent rate. Capital gains—either in the form of mutual fund distributions or the sale of appreciated stock—may be taxed at either rate. Gains on stocks held for a year or longer are taxed at 15 percent; gains on stocks held for less than a year are taxed at ordinary tax rates. You can exploit this differing tax treatment by wisely allocating your assets among your tax-deferred accounts (such as IRAs, 401(k)s, and annuities) and your taxable accounts (pretty much everything else). Tax-efficient investments like municipal bonds and individual stocks should be held in your taxable accounts. Investments that generate distributions subject to ordinary income tax (such as taxable bonds, CDs, and REITs) should be held in tax-deferred accounts.

Keep in mind that these are general guidelines, not hard and fast rules. Clearly you will need to keep some tax-inefficient money in your taxable accounts. The point is simply to recognize that you have a choice and can make decisions that will reduce your tax bill. The final thing you can do to lower your tax-related expenses is to properly sequence withdrawals from your accounts. In the vast majority of cases, you should allow your tax-deferred money to grow for as long as possible. That's because any withdrawals will be taxed as ordinary income. Money you withdraw from taxable accounts is not taxable, unless you realize a gain as part of the transaction.

Navigating the ABCs of Mutual Fund Share Prices

Mutual fund companies are in business to make money, and that's absolutely acceptable. That, after all, is the American way. And like most companies, they offer their products in a variety of forms and at a variety of price points. So just as Apple offers its ubiquitous iPod in Nano, Shuffle, Classic, and Touch configurations, mutual fund companies offer their investment management services in different "share classes," each with decidedly different cost structures. What's different from the iPod analogy, however, is that the consumer usually doesn't get a chance to compare features and benefits. In fact, in many cases, the consumer doesn't even know that the other share classes are available. The other key difference is that consumers who buy the iPod Touch are getting a product that is clearly superior in all meaningful ways to the iPod Shuffle—and they are willing to pay a premium price for that superiority. With mutual fund share classes, however, there is no difference—*no difference at all*—between the offerings except for the premium price. Unlike any other products or services we can think of, the more expensive the mutual fund share class the more inferior the quality and value.

Let's take a look at a real example from a real fund company—the Equity Income Fund from Fidelity Investments. We're not doing this to pick on them because Fidelity is right up there with Vanguard, T. Rowe Price, and American Funds as a company that truly strives to do the right thing for its shareholders. Nonetheless, the following table demonstrates that no one—and no company—is perfect.

Fees Matter	
Fund Name	**Expense**
Fidelity Equity Income Fund	0.66
Fidelity Advisor Equity Income Fund A	0.97
Fidelity Advisor Equity Income Fund T	1.18
Fidelity Advisor Equity Income Fund C	1.73
Fidelity Advisor Equity Income Fund B	1.79

The Fidelity Equity Income Fund is a standard large-cap U.S. stock fund. It falls into the "Value" category of the Morningstar style box grid, meaning that it holds stocks that are considered under-valued relative to the broad market. Like all mutual funds, it charges a fee for portfolio management, fund administration, and the like. In the case of the no-load shares, which are readily available for direct investment by any-one, the fees are quite reasonable—totaling 66 basis points. That means for every $100 you invest in this fund, Fidelity charges 66 cents a year. That also means the fund has to earn 66 cents on your $100 for you to break even. In the big picture that's a pretty reasonable price.

But here's where it gets really ugly. You take that same Fidelity fund—with the same portfolio manager, the same investment strategy, and the same holdings—and you can pay some very different prices. First off you'll notice that the fund name is slightly different. The word *Advisor* has been added. That means these share classes are sold by the registered representatives of a broker-dealer like Merrill Lynch or Smith Barney. The operative word is *sold,* because the brokers are compensated for every dollar their clients invest in these funds. Here's how the Fidelity Website describes the Advisor series of funds:

> Fidelity Advisor funds are a family of 90-plus mutual funds available to investors only through investment professionals. Funds range from conservative and tax-advantaged income funds to aggressive growth and sector funds. Fidelity Advisor Funds can provide your business with greater pricing flexibility with A, B, C, I, and T shares. This allows you to select a load structure that best reflects the needs and preferences of each individual client.

Please re-read that last sentence: The Advisor funds allow *the broker* to "select a load structure that best reflects the needs and preferences of each individual client." Though Fidelity does its best to make this selection process sound fair and altruistic, in reality most investors have no idea what they're being sold and, if they did indeed have a preference, it would clearly be for the share class with the lowest possible cost. In the vast majority of cases, this type of multi-class pricing is designed to address the needs and preferences of the broker—not the client.

Taking another look at the table, you'll see that, in the case of the A-shares, you'll be charged 97 cents annually for each 100 dollars you have invested in the fund. Unfortunately, that doesn't tell the whole story. A-shares also carry a "front-end load" that usually averages 5 percent but can be as high as 7 percent or 8 percent. Using that same example, if you invest $100 in an A-share mutual fund only $95 will actually make it into the fund; the other $5 goes to the broker. As a result, in the first year, you'll pay $5.97 in expenses—$0.97 to Fidelity and $5.00 to the broker. And just what benefit does that extra 5 percent buy you? Depends on whom you ask. If you ask us, there is no benefit. If you ask the mutual fund companies and the brokers selling these products, they'll tell you that the load compensates the "investment professional" for his or her expertise in evaluating and recommending the appropriate funds for their clients. What they don't tell you, however, is that—for all this professional analysis and oversight—load funds do not outperform their no-load counterparts. And a big reason for that is the higher expense ratio.

Next up are the T-shares that come in at 118 basis points or $1.18 per $100. Like the A-shares, however, the T-shares also assess a front-end load so that 118 basis point expense ratio is somewhat misleading.

And then we get into the truly silly zone. The Fidelity Advisor Equity Income C-shares have an annual expense charge of 173 basis points and the B-shares charge 179 basis points. But, wait, because that's not all. B-shares also feature what's known as a "contingent deferred sales charge" (typically reduced to its "CDSC" acronym). So while you don't pay an upfront load, you will be assessed a backend charge if you decide to sell the fund during the surrender-charge period that usually runs five to 10 years and typically begins at 5 percent or 6 percent. C-shares also feature a CDSC, but the surrender charged is fixed at 1 percent and disappears after you've held the fund for one full year.

So why would anyone choose a B- or C-share mutual fund? Why would they start every year knowing they had to earn almost a 2-percent return just to break even? And why, in the first year, would they knowingly put themselves 5 percent in the hole? Because they don't know, they don't know to ask and, sadly, their broker is not telling them the whole story.

Active vs. Passive Mutual Funds—Fees vs. Performance

From its very inception in 1924, the huge mutual fund industry has been predicated on the belief that individual portfolio managers can out-think, out-smart, and out-perform the overall stock market. In essence, the industry believes that the markets are inefficient and that crack portfolio managers can capture that inefficiency and convert it into outsized profits. The industry still clings to that belief, but the facts prove otherwise.

The next three tables compare the performance of actively managed mutual funds against their benchmarks (or indices). The tables specify the percentage of funds that *failed* to beat their benchmark, so the higher the percentage the worse the funds did. The information is for the period ending December 31, 2008, and is provided for one-, three-, and five-year periods. You can see the significant under-performance for each time period, but pay particular attention to the one-year numbers representing calendar year 2008. We say that because advocates of active management argue that their approach will protect investors in down markets because they aren't locked into a fixed allocation like index funds are. The results do not support that premise.

This first table compares U.S. equity funds to their respective benchmark. Large-cap value is the only asset class that managed to beat the benchmark, and it did so even in 2008. The rest of the table makes a convincing argument to stick with index funds.

Percentage of U.S. Equity Funds Outperformed by Benchmarks			
Fund Category	One-Year	Three-Year	Five-Year
Large-Cap Growth	89.95	88.42	80.51
Large-Cap Value	22.17	35.80	53.19
Mid-Cap Growth	88.95	68.75	76.58
Mid-Cap Value	67.06	78.26	79.17
Small-Cap Growth	95.50	81.87	95.58
Small-Cap Value	72.55	63.16	69.51
Source: Standard & Poor's.			

The story with international equity is similar. International small-cap funds matched or outperformed the benchmark for the one- and three-year periods. Everyone else did quite poorly.

Percentage of International Equity Funds Outperformed by Benchmarks			
Fund Category	One-Year	Three-Year	Five-Year
Global	59.83	64.04	63.16
International	63.96	76.52	83.52
International Small-Cap	50.00	48.84	58.82
Emerging Markets	65.06	83.93	89.83
Source: Standard & Poor's.			

But here's the big story. With the exception of high-yield bond funds, fixed-income funds got trounced by their benchmarks. In the table on page 75 you'll actually see several instances where 100 percent of the active funds underperformed the benchmark. In truth, this should not be surprising. It all comes back to the issue of fees and expenses. Bond fund portfolio managers have fewer opportunities than their equity counterparts to truly add "alpha"—or out-performance based on their bond selection and trading activities. Unlike stocks, bonds do not have the potential to double or triple in value. So most bond funds perform pretty much the same, with their all-in-fees being the primary differentiator. If that's the case, and this table provides compelling evidence, go with the lowest cost bond fund to get the highest possible return.

When you consider all this data in the aggregate, you're left with only two possible reasons for the dismal performance of active mutual funds. Either the portfolio managers aren't as smart as they think they are, or the expenses charged by actively managed funds are simply too high. We believe both reasons contribute to the dismal results, but expenses constitute the primary culprit. Think about it this way: Let's say the market actually is inefficient. The question remains *how* inefficient is it? If it is 1-percent or 2-percent inefficient (and it would be difficult to argue for a larger degree of inefficiency in today's world of instant communications), and the portfolio manager is able to capture *all* of that inefficiency, he or she would still trail the market because the fund's stated expenses would rapidly and rapaciously eat up that profit.

Stated expenses, however, are only part of the problem with actively managed funds. Indeed, you could argue that stated expenses are merely the tip of the proverbial iceberg when it comes to what shareholders actually pay. In their 2007 research paper, "Scale Effects in Mutual Fund Performance: The Role of Trading Costs," Roger Edelen, Richard Evans of Boston College, and Gregory Kadlec of Virginia Tech

Percentage of Fixed-Income Funds Outperformed by Benchmarks

Fund Category	One-Year	Three-Year	Five-Year
Government Long	89.90	93.33	92.68
Government Intermediate	91.30	91.11	93.75
Government Short	84.21	91.43	91.43
Investment-Grade Long	94.79	94.74	100.00
Investment-Grade Intermediate	90.14	91.18	90.18
Investment-Grade Short	98.72	100.00	100.00
High Yield	37.04	43.75	52.29
Mortgage-Backed Securities	93.75	100.00	100.00
Global Income	78.13	86.36	79.07
Emerging Markets Debt	65.22	68.75	62.50
General Municipal Debt	80.56	84.72	95.89

Source: Standard & Poor's.

determined that shareholders annually pay (that is, lose) another 1.44 percent of their investment dollars to cover the costs incurred by mutual fund portfolio managers buying and selling securities. These costs represent commissions on each buy-sell transaction, the spread between the bid-ask price for each security, and the market impact cost that results when large blocks of a particular security are traded (driving up the price if the fund is buying, and driving the price down if the fund is selling). Interestingly, in an interview for the Boston College alumni magazine, Edelen observed that, in general, fund managers were pretty good about their buy and sell decisions. The problem, however, is that their "skills are swamped by their implementation costs, so that, on net, shareholders find themselves behind the starting line."

The strongest argument against index funds and in favor of active management centers on the portfolio managers ability to be nimble and defensive in times of market downturns. They're supposed to be able to hoard cash and deploy it on defensive stock picks that can better withstand the pain of a crushing bear market. If that's true then there was never a better time for active managers to shine than in 2008. From our standpoint, actively managed mutual funds had their opportunity to shine, and they failed miserably. If you want your money to work as hard as possible, build a portfolio that uses low-cost index funds. If you do choose to use actively managed funds, select ones with low expense ratios and/or ones whose portfolio managers have demonstrated unusual skill in their particular niche.

Final Proof

If you're still not convinced that fees matter when it comes to your investment choices, consider this graphic. You've just received an inheritance of $100,000. You decide to invest $50,000 each in two different funds. Fund A has an expense ratio of 1.30 percent; Fund B has an expense ratio of 0.30 percent. Over a 25-year period, both funds deliver the same 8-percent rate of return. At the end of the 25-year period, the 1.0-percent difference in annual costs—or the average difference between an index fund and an actively managed fund—yielded an extra $66,443 in Fund B.

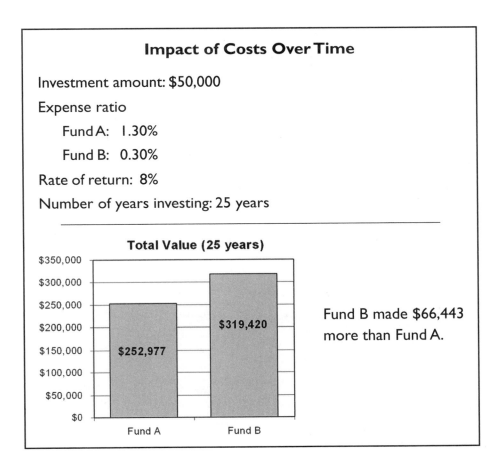

Impact of Costs Over Time

Investment amount: $50,000

Expense ratio

    Fund A: 1.30%

    Fund B: 0.30%

Rate of return: 8%

Number of years investing: 25 years

Total Value (25 years)

Fund A: $252,977

Fund B: $319,420

Fund B made $66,443 more than Fund A.

So it's your choice. Would you rather feel smart about purchasing the "dumb" index fund or feel dumb about purchasing the "smart" active fund?

Chapter 5

I NFLATIONARY:
Keeping Pace With the Cost of Living

Inflation is probably the most dangerous threat to enjoying a comfortable retirement and, as such, it is a critically important consideration in building an effective Nest Egg Game Plan. Interestingly, of all the things that affect the creation of a lifetime income stream, inflation is the most widely known and understood (on the surface, at least), but it is also the most ignored. Inflation often lurks as the proverbial "elephant in the room" that no one wants to recognize or discuss. But denying the impact of inflation is a deal-breaker. You need to accept its presence and address its long-term effects or suffer its consequences.

Inflation represents a double-edged sword for retirees. It forces you to withdraw greater amounts from your savings and investment accounts to keep up with rising prices, while at the same time the intrinsic value of your assets is shrinking. Think of it as the polar opposite to the concept of dollar cost averaging that works so well during the accumulation phase. Instead of buying more when prices are low, inflation forces you to sell more when prices are low. And unlike during your working years, there is little opportunity to make up for any shortfalls.

The insidious nature of inflation also stems from its relatively slow creep. It sneaks up on us so we often don't feel its full impact until the damage is irreversible. Part of the problem is that the Department of Labor typically reports inflation numbers on a calendar-year basis. So, on a year-over-year basis, we'll hear that inflation is running in the range of 2 percent or 3 percent, and that doesn't sound particularly onerous. But just as the power of compound interest helps accelerate our savings, the effects of compounded inflation rates are dramatic. Here's how it works. If you assume a 3-percent annual inflation rate, then something that costs $10.00 at the beginning of the year would cost $10.30 at the end of the first year, $10.61 after two years, $11.60 after just five years, and $13.44 after 10 years. What seemed like a benign ripple in our income stream has quickly turned into a deadly tidal wave.

The charts that follow on pages 81 and 82 provide three different views of inflation: year-by-year inflation rates since 1926, the cumulative rate of inflation over that time period, and the resulting decrease in the purchasing power of a dollar.

The second chart on page 81 shows how the cumulative effect of inflation would effectively increase the price of an item that cost $1 in 1926 to $11.73 in 2008.

This last chart shown on page 82 is the one to focus on because it drives home the danger of inflation during retirement. And inflation is indeed far more dangerous and painful during retirement. When you're working, your wages tend to increase with inflation so you can usually maintain a consistent standard of living. When you're retired, however,

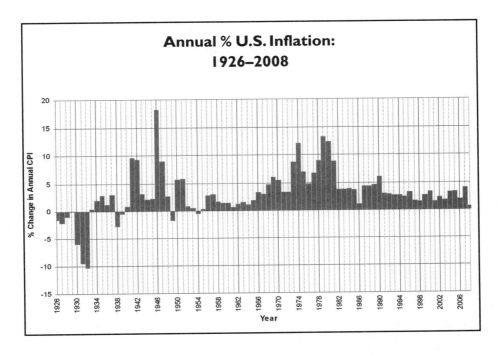

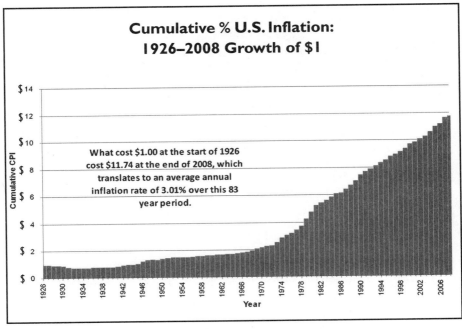

cost-of-living adjustments are relatively rare—except for Social Security payments. Income generated from 401(k) plans, IRAs, annuities, CDs, bonds, and the like is not adjusted for inflation. That means you have to plan for and accommodate inflation in Your Nest Egg Game Plan. Although that is easier said than done, it is not impossible, and the remainder of this chapter will outline how to accomplish that goal.

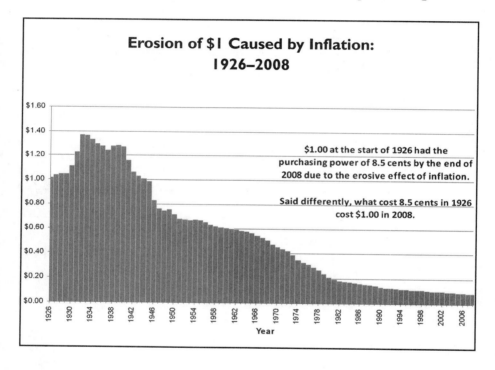

Erosion of $1 Caused by Inflation: 1926–2008

$1.00 at the start of 1926 had the purchasing power of 8.5 cents by the end of 2008 due to the erosive effect of inflation.

Said differently, what cost 8.5 cents in 1926 cost $1.00 in 2008.

But First the Bad News

Most people believe that inflation is a simple concept measured by the well-known Consumer Price Index (CPI). In reality, it is far more complicated than that. The U.S. Bureau of Labor Statistics actually calculates four different inflation indices:

1. The CPI measures the average price change of a wide variety of goods and services in different parts of the country. It provides the broadest view of inflation.

2. The CPI-U measures the spending habits and price changes for American consumers living in urban areas. The CPI-U represents approximately 87 percent of the U.S. population.

3. The CPI-W measures price changes for residents of urban areas who work in clerical or hourly wage occupations. It's a subset of the CPI-U and represents 32 percent of the U.S population.

4. And then there's the CPI-E that reflects the inflation rate experienced by people 62 years of age and older. The CPI-E represents 16 percent of the population. (It should be noted that the CPI-E was created in 1987 as an "experimental index," whatever that means, and still carries that caveat to this day.)

The key difference between the CPI-E and the broader traditional indices is the relative weighting given to certain goods and services. As a result, this inflationary measure for older Americans has moved at a different rate than the other indices. From 1982 to 2007, the CPI-E rose 126.5 percent, versus increases of 115.2 percent for the CPI-U and 110 percent for the CPI-W. The bottom line is that, during the last quarter century, older Americans have had to deal with higher inflation rates than the broader population. This difference is due largely to the fact that the elderly spend a substantially higher percentage of their budget on medical care, shelter, and fuel oil than does the broader population. And price increases in all three of those categories— medical care, shelter, and fuel oil—outpaced the overall inflation rate.

So what's the bad news? The cost of living adjustments to Social Security payments are based on the CPI-W, not the CPI-E (probably because the Social Security system couldn't handle the increased benefit costs associated with higher COLA increases). Whatever the reason, the key takeaway is that you shouldn't count on Social Security as the sole inflationary hedge in your Nest Egg Game Plan.

Additional Inflationary Factors to Consider

Average inflation rates can also vary dramatically based on several other factors, including:

- **Geography:** During the last 10 years, for example, inflation has averaged 2.3 percent in Atlanta, compared to 3.5 percent in San Diego. Retirees who decide to settle down in rural communities and enjoy low-cost recreational pursuits like hiking, fishing, and cycling will experience inflation rates close to the national average. Retirees who opt for a more cosmopolitan location will find that their income does not go quite as far.

- **Social class:** As politically incorrect as it may sound, upper-class pursuits tend to increase in price far faster than mass-market activities and products. Part of this is due to the "Walmart factor" that tends to drive down the price of the more generic staples of American life. Nordstrom's and Tiffany tend to be somewhat immune from this trend, as are luxury car-makers like BMW and Mercedes, which have increased the prices of their automobiles at a much faster clip than Ford and Chevrolet. With the dramatic loss in wealth caused by the global economic meltdown of 2008, the "inflation premium" of luxury providers will likely wilt.

- **Gender:** A recent Merrill Lynch study indicated that the inflation rate for females is more than 3 percent, while it's less than 1 percent for males. The difference, again, is one's spending habits—primarily the fact that women's overall healthcare costs are as much as 30-percent higher than men's, and they pay a higher percentage (19 percent vs. 16 percent) of their healthcare expenses out-of-pocket.

Inflation-Fighting Investments

It sounds counter-intuitive but, on an inflation-adjusted basis, some of the "safest" fixed-income investments may be the most dangerous for people living on a fixed income. Here's why. Let's say you buy a

$100,000 20-year Treasury bond backed by the full faith and credit of the U.S. government. From a pure principal-protection standpoint, this is the least-risky investment in the world. Let's further assume that the bond has a 5-percent yield. That means you will receive $5,000 per year in interest payments and, at the end of 20 years, you'll get your $100,000 back. What you won't get back, however, is $100,000 of purchasing power. If you assume a 3-percent inflation rate, the purchasing power of your original investment will have shrunk to $55,367. In addition, the purchasing power of each interest payment will also decline—with the final $5,000 payment being worth only $2,768 in constant dollars. Keep in mind that the same issues apply to corporate bonds, bank CDs, and most other fixed rate-of-return investment options.

The second inflation-related concern about fixed-income investments, in addition to the loss of purchasing power, is that yields are always quoted on a "nominal basis," not as a "real return." What's the difference? Nominal returns, or the stated interest rate, reflect the compensation you will receive for loaning your money to the particular issuer. As with the previous example, if you invest $100,000 at a nominal rate of return of 5 percent, you'll earn $5,000 per year. The real return on your investment, however, could vary dramatically depending on the then-current inflation rate. If inflation is at 0 percent, then your real return will be 5 percent, the same as the nominal rate. If inflation is running at 3 percent, then your real return is only 2 percent. And if inflation were to rise above 5 percent, you would actually have a negative return on your investment.

So if the principal-protection safety of fixed-income investments brings with it the danger of low or negative real-returns, what can you do to protect your portfolio from the ravages of inflation? The following five asset classes can provide an inflationary hedge to help keep pace with rising prices:

1. **Common Stock:** Over the long term, stock investments have been effective inflation fighters. That's because companies can raise prices for their products when their costs increase during inflationary periods. These higher prices will often translate into higher earnings and, as a result, higher share prices. The flipside is that, over shorter time periods, inflation can negatively impact earnings and share prices. Despite these short-term risks, stocks should constitute a core element of your inflation-fighting portfolio.

2. **Inflation-Indexed Bonds:** The U.S. government introduced Treasury Inflation-Protected Securities (more commonly known as TIPS) in 1997. TIPS combine the safety of U.S. Treasuries with an interest rate and underlying principal amount that both adjust to reflect changes in the CPI. So, unlike a traditional government or corporate bond that simply returns your principal at maturity, TIPS offer an opportunity for an inflation-linked upside. For example, if you purchase a $10,000 TIP, at maturity you might receive $10,500, $11,000, or more depending on the extent of inflation during the bond's life. And that's in addition to receiving the semi-annual interest payments, which were also adjusted for inflation. Keep in mind that the price for this protection is a relatively low yield. In addition, you need to be careful when investing in TIPS because any increases in principal value are immediately taxable as reportable income despite the fact that you won't truly realize the gain until maturity. Because of this "phantom tax" treatment, TIPS should only be owned in tax-deferred accounts.

3. **Floating-Rate Bank Notes:** In simplest terms these are bond-like instruments with a yield tied to a specified market rate, typically LIBOR (the London Inter-Bank Offered Rate) or the federal funds rate, plus a spread. For example, the yield might be expressed as "LIBOR plus 50 basis points." That means if LIBOR is at 4.0 percent, the notes will yield 4.5 percent. If LIBOR goes up to 5.0 percent, the notes will yield 5.5 percent. Floating-rate notes have

virtually no interest-rate risk and are a particularly good choice when rates are increasing, as happens during inflationary periods. Their disadvantage is that many floating-rate notes are at the lower end of the investment quality spectrum and are riskier than government bonds and investment grade corporates. If you like the idea of a variable yield that could keep pace with inflation, consider accessing this asset class via a mutual fund or ETF.

4. **Real Estate:** Despite the beating that real estate has endured in recent years, it remains an effective long-term hedge against inflation. And although direct ownership of investment property is one approach to real estate exposure, most investors would be better served by the considerably more diversified and liquid approach offered by REIT (that is, real estate investment trust) mutual funds and ETFs. Real estate provides two inflationary benefits. The first is that most REITs can offset inflation by charging higher rents via escalation clauses or when leases become due. And second, because REITs represent "real assets" they tend to increase in value along with inflation. REITs are also valuable to retirees because of their high dividend stream. By law, U.S. REITs must pay out at least 90 percent of their taxable income to shareholders. Over the period from 1986 to 2008, REIT dividends averaged 7.4 percent annually. Like everything in life and investing, all is not rosy with REITs. Unlike corporate dividends, much of the income generated by REITs is taxable at ordinary income rates rather than the 15-percent dividend tax rate. In addition, REITs are just as volatile as stocks and experienced a 37-percent decline in value during 2008. Notwithstanding that volatility, REITs are a good choice for a small allocation in most income-generating portfolios.

5. **Commodities:** Gold has been the traditional inflation hedge and remains so today, but it's no longer the only game in town. With so much media attention given to the alternative investing strategies

of portfolio managers like David Swensen who runs the Yale University endowment, compounded with the horrific performance of the stock market, there's been a huge inflow of investment dollars into asset classes representing basic materials and mining, agricultural products, oil and gas, timber, and precious metals. The reason is twofold. These kinds of assets typically rise in price along with inflation, and they typically have a low correlation to the stock market. The operative word, however, is *typically*. These asset classes are anything but typical. They are among the most volatile investments available to individuals. Nonetheless, they can make a good addition to a retirement portfolio—but make sure to limit your exposure to 5 percent or less.

The Inflationary Bottom Line

Inflation is unavoidable, but it need not be terrifying. In reality, the opposite of inflation, "deflation," is far more troublesome. Deflation refers to a steady fall in prices and, when lasting over a sustained period of time, often results in depressions such as occurred in the 1930s. (Disinflation, on the other hand, refers to a period when inflation is present but in steady decline.)

Like every other aspect of investing and income generation, inflation represents a risk that simply needs to be recognized and accommodated. Build it into your plan and your plan can work. Ignore it, and your plan will collapse like a house of cards in a wind tunnel.

Chapter 6

I NTROSPECTIVE:
Knowing Yourself

The best piece of advice Phil ever received in his career was that he should "begin at the end." Rather than approaching work one day at a time, Phil's mentor advised him to look down the road and plan his legacy. The idea was to make believe you're 20 years in the future, looking back on what you've accomplished. What exactly do you hope to see and, most importantly, how do you want to feel about the last 20 years? This type of visualization helps crystallize your goals and helps keep you on track by ensuring that everything you do moves you one step closer to making that visualized dream a reality.

This same advice works well for retirees. National averages and third-party opinions are meaningless when it comes to determining the driving factors of one's happiness. That's true during one's working years, and it's especially true in retirement. Your retirement life stage is only successful if it provides a sense of satisfaction and comfort—as defined by you and you alone.

This book is focused on the financial aspects of retirement—how to make your nest egg generate enough income to last your lifetime. And without question, the size and income-generating power of your nest egg are critical components of a successful retirement plan, but in reality the size of your nest egg does not tell the whole story. Retirements can fall short of one's dreams for non-financial reasons as well. So it's wise to take a step back, do some soul-searching, and create a retirement life-plan as well as a financial plan.

The first step in that process is to truly know yourself—perhaps for the very first time. Without getting all schmaltzy, Henry David Thoreau's classic quote "the mass of men lead lives of quiet desperation" could appropriately be updated for the 21st century as "the mass of men (and women) speed through their lives in an information-overloaded, time-pressed fog." We often spend so much time worrying about our jobs, our kids, and our aging parents that we forget to spend quality time with our spouses and quality time alone. When you retire, a lot of the stuff that kept you occupied during your working years will be gone. Instead of rushing to catch the train to work, rushing through breakfast, lunch, and dinner, and rushing to get your kids to soccer and band practice on time, you'll be rushing to...?

That, of course, is the key question: Where will you be rushing? What exactly is your retirement destination? The critical component of a happy and fulfilling retirement is the realization that you're not retiring *from* something; you're retiring *to* something. And the something you're retiring to may last longer than what you're retiring from. It's become a cliché to say that life is a journey, but it's a cliché because it's true. That journey continues through retirement, and the truly beautiful thing about the retirement leg of the journey is that you can set your own pace and your own direction. You're the boss.

But being the boss means responsibility and accountability. If you mess it up, you have no one to blame but yourself. Here's how to not mess it up.

An Introspective Checklist

We are big fans of writing things down. Sharing stories, anecdotes, and gut feelings are important, but nothing gets you focused like putting pen to paper does. Simply thinking about one's retirement can too easily veer off into daydreaming and a procession of "happy thoughts" that have no connection to reality. So begin your process of self-discovery by asking yourself a series of questions and recording your answers in pixels or print. (If you're part of couple, do this exercise individually and then share your responses.)

> ▷ What will you miss most about not working full-time?
>
> ▷ What will you not miss?
>
> ▷ What are the skills you're most proud of and most enjoy using?
>
> ▷ How can you put those skills to work in new and enjoyable ways during retirement?
>
> ▷ What activities make you happiest?
>
> ▷ If you had to write a eulogy for yourself—based solely on how you lived your life during retirement—what would you say?
>
> ▷ What avocation, hobby, or other type of pleasurable pursuit did you abandon during your working years that you would like to pursue again?
>
> ▷ Who are the people you want to stay close to or reconnect with?
>
> ▷ Your fondest memories are of what and whom?
>
> ▷ Is there a commonality among those fond memories?
>
> ▷ Do you have a "bucket list" (or a list of things you'd like to accomplish or experience before you pass away)? If not, should you create one?

> ⊳ What is the one indulgence you cannot live without?

> ⊳ What is the one vice you will strive to live without?

> ⊳ What would you like to learn?

> ⊳ What would you like to teach so others can learn from you?

There are hundreds of similar questions that you can and should ask and answer, but, rather than try to address them all, the remainder of this chapter will focus on some of the key questions that face every pre- or post-retiree.

Where Should I Live?

This is the big one: Should I stay in my existing house, move nearby to a smaller house, or move to an entirely different part of the country or the world? It's the question that most people grapple with at some point before or during retirement. It's the question that often causes friction between couples. And it's the question that everyone you know has an opinion about. Politely tell them to keep their opinions to themselves. This is your retirement.

In general, retirees relocate for one of several reasons. They:

> ⊳ Downsize for personal reasons (the house is too big for empty-nesters) and either stay close to their original home or move elsewhere.

> ⊳ Downsize for financial reasons (they cash out, and buy or rent something less expensive) and stay close to home or move away.

> ⊳ Move closer to someone (children, siblings, or friends) or something (the country, the city, the ocean, or a more temperate climate).

It would be easy to categorize the first two reasons for relocating as the result of quantitative and dispassionate decision-making, while labeling the third as highly personal, subjective, and emotional. In truth, there is nothing dispassionate about moving out of one's home— regardless of when or why. To paraphrase the MasterCard commercial, a house has a specific dollar value but a home is priceless. Too many people allow the financial investment in their home to take precedence over their emotional investment. And although bad financial investments can often be righted over time, poor emotional investments may be impossible to undo and can haunt you forever.

The decision to stay or move should not be an impulsive one. It's a decision you should be evaluating and preparing for several years prior to finalizing. There is no need to rush. Your retirement is likely to last 20, 30, or 40 years, so there is no need to have every aspect of your retirement life finalized on day one. Life—whether while working or in retirement—isn't like that. The smartest decision might be to make no decision at all when you first retire. Instead, see how you feel about retirement in safe and familiar surroundings. The first years of retirement are akin to a socio-economic lab experiment. Introducing too many variables will cloud your understanding of cause and effect, and what's important. If you move as soon as you retire and find yourself restless and discontented, is it because you miss your home, your work, your old neighborhood, your friends, or any of the countless other interactions and experiences we associate with our day-to-day lives? Would you have been equally restless and discontent if you had stayed put? The bottom line is that there is no need to put yourself in such a tenuous circumstance immediately upon retirement. At one key level, retirement is a time to "chill out," so start by chilling out at home with the friends and environment you already know.

A surprisingly large percentage of people make relocation decisions based on a modicum of information. Countless people have moved to a new location without ever having lived there for an extended period of time. It's seems self-evident that moving to Florida, just because you always enjoyed your wintertime vacations in Ft. Myers, doesn't mean you'll be happy there in the summer. And though the slow pace of northern Vermont or Cape Cod may be just what the doctor ordered for your annual two-week vacation, that slow pace may very well drive you nuts for 52 weeks a year. You absolutely should begin your investigation of potential relocation areas with short-term vacations and visits, but don't make your decision based on that experience. Rent an apartment for a year and experience all four seasons. If it still feels like the place you want to live, then begin the process of moving. If it doesn't, then simply repeat the vetting process elsewhere.

Relocating anywhere is a big step, and way too many retirees allow emotions to cloud their decision-making process. Phil's parents provide a good illustration of how not to make a relocation decision. Jo and Mike Fragasso were lifetime New Yorkers. Born and bred there. Their only child, Phil, went to college in Boston and settled there after graduation. Most of Jo's family—her mother, brothers, and sisters— and all of their friends lived within a 20-minute drive from their Long Island home. Nonetheless, when Mike retired, they decided to move to Connecticut—precisely halfway between their family and friends and their son. They bought a condo in a new community in central Connecticut, where they knew no one, and were now about a two-and-a-half-hour drive from everyone they cared about. In their mind they figured they were close enough to Boston that Phil would regularly drive down for Sunday dinner, and their friends and family would love to drive to the Connecticut countryside to visit. The problem is that the New York–to-Connecticut-to-Boston drive is among the most congested to be found anywhere. And for Mike and Jo to visit their family and friends, they either had to drive through New York City or take a ferry across the Long Island Sound. Either route was long, tiring, and expensive. The Connecticut experiment lasted less than 18 months and they moved back to their own stomping grounds, which they never should have left in the first place.

Despite the title of this section, "Where Should I Live?," the concept of "should" plays no role in deciding where to live. The real questions to answer are "where do I want to live?," "where will I be happiest?," and "where will I have the greatest chance to make my Nest Egg Game Plan successful?"

What Lifestyle Do I Want and/or Need?

This is another key area where people often get tripped up. They sometimes try to emulate others (for example, my cousin Suzie volunteers at the library so maybe I will as well) rather than discovering the activities and pursuits that they can truly be passionate about. Every stage of life requires some lifestyle decision-making. And while these decisions are not carved in stone, they do have a significant impact on your happiness and fulfillment—especially in retirement, when your work-life routine is not there to balance off or otherwise complement your leisure routine. To better visualize and prepare for your retirement lifestyle, consider these kinds of questions:

> - Do you plan to travel extensively, moderately, or almost never? Where will you travel? How long will your trips last? Are you more likely to rent a small apartment and live in Rome for three months or be part of a tour group that buses through Europe visiting one city a day?

> - Are you more likely to buy an RV or buy into a retirement community?

> - Do you want to stay close to your children and grandchildren?

> - Given the choice, would you prefer to work part-time, start a new business, go back to school, volunteer, or focus solely on leisure activities?

> - Are your recreational activities inexpensive (such as reading, hiking, cycling, or painting) or expensive (for example, golfing, boating, or antique collecting)?

> ▷ What kinds of things or activities do you tend to splurge on (for example, new cars, eating out, clothing, or vacations)?

> ▷ Is it important that you leave a financial legacy to your heirs or a charity? If so, how much do you want to leave and how much of a financial sacrifice are you willing to make to accomplish this charitable goal?

> ▷ Does your medical history—and the histories of your parents, grandparents, and siblings—raise any red flags or concerns that might affect your short-term or long-term retirement lifestyle?

How Much Will I Need?

We talked a lot about the overly simplistic and somewhat misleading concept of "the number" in Chapter 2, but it's worth revisiting because the key variable in determining a so-called number is you and what you want your retirement to look like and feel like. And because the key number is not the lump sum you'll need at retirement, you need to focus on the truly critical number of how much money you'll need each and every year.

The first step is to make believe today is the first day of your retirement. Look out over the next 12 months and determine how much money you would need to live comfortably and contentedly. Start with your fixed expenses (housing, property taxes, insurance, and healthcare), move on to your variable costs (car loans, utilities, groceries, fuel, clothing, home repairs, and income tax), and conclude with expenses that are truly discretionary (eating out, travel, hobbies, sports, entertainment, and charitable contributions). Add it all up and that's your income-need number for today. After adjusting your income-need number by the amount of Social Security and/or corporate pension payments you expect to receive, compare the resulting income-need number to the total of your savings and investment accounts. If the income-need number equals less than 5 percent of your investment balance, you're in good shape. If the income-need numbers is closer to 7 percent or 8 percent of your investment balance, you really need to take a close look at the numbers. Any withdrawal need higher than 8 percent is cause for serious pause and should force you to investigate ways to reduce your expenses or increase your income in both the short-term and long-term.

Repeat the exercise at the beginning of every single year. It will force you to rethink your priorities to ensure a lifetime stream of income. The rest of your life is always in the future, and you always have an opportunity to live it to the fullest while living within your means.

Investing Introspective

In addition to the quality-of-life types of questions we reviewed earlier, you need to also give careful consideration to a host of investment-related issues. The key question is whether you are a hands-on investor who closely monitors the market's every move or whether you prefer to turn over the reins to a professional financial advisor? Investing, like most specialties, is not rocket science. Anyone with interest, time, and discipline can be a successful investor. If you possess all three of those attributes, you should be fine managing the financial part of your Nest Egg Game Plan on your own. If not, find yourself an investment advisor with low fees and low-cost investment options. If you're undecided, ask yourself these questions. Your answers will guide you to the investing approach that's right for you.

> ▹ Do you tend to panic when the market goes down or suffer from "irrational exuberance" when it jumps?

> ▹ Do you understand the trade-off between risk and reward?

> ▹ Do you understand the differences between market risk, credit risk, inflation risk, principal risk, and liquidity risk?

▷ Does your current investment portfolio reflect these risks appropriately?

▷ Do you understand every holding in your portfolio, and can you explain, in 10 words or less, why you own each?

▷ Do you have both a buy strategy and a sell strategy?

▷ How do approach asset allocation and rebalancing? Do you rebalance on a calendar basis or with a rules-based strategy?

▷ Has your past success with investing been the result of luck or a carefully thought-out strategy?

▷ If you're part of a couple and something happens to you, will your surviving partner need assistance maintaining your investment strategy?

Non-Working Activity Assessment

This simple exercise will help identify and rank your non-work activities in terms of how much time you devote to them and how much enjoyment and personal satisfaction you derive from them. The result will provide a unique, graphical snapshot of how you spend your leisure time today, and how that might change in the years to come.

The first step is to list 10 to 25 specific activities you're engaged in when not working. These should range from chores (housework, car repairs, and cooking) to recreation (golf, fishing, scrapbooking, or playing cards) to personal time (reading, writing, walking, or painting) to spiritual time (praying, attending church service, or volunteering) to pure leisure (watching television, listening to music, talking with friends).

On the following grid, plot each of these activities in terms of how much time you dedicate to them and the value they provide in terms of joy and self-satisfaction.

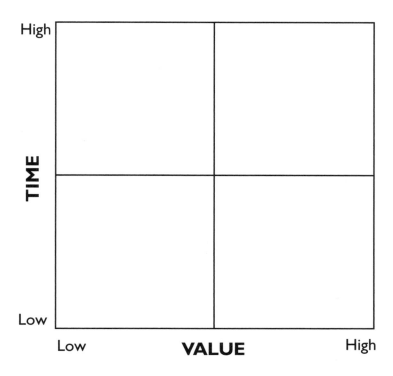

After you've plotted your list of activities, take a look at the grid from a purely graphical standpoint. Ignore the names of the activities and, instead, concentrate on how they are spread among the four quadrants. Ideally, you want everything to fall in the upper right-hand box (a lot of time on high-value activities) and the bottom left-hand box (very little time on low-value activities). What you don't want to be doing is spending a lot of time on low-value activities or very little time on high-value activities. If you find a lot of activities located in the upper left-hand box and the lower right-hand box, consider ways to allocate more or less time to those activities. Clearly, it is impossible to eliminate all of your time-consuming non-fulfilling activities (such as cleaning the toilet and washing the kitchen floor), but it is usually quite easy to become more efficient at those non-fulfilling tasks to free up more time for the joy-giving parts of your life.

Chapter 7

INSPIRED:
Making Your Dreams Come True

A key element of a successful Nest Egg Game Plan is the deeply felt belief that you are retiring *to* something, not *from* something. However you define that something you're retiring to, it should be inspired and, on occasion, indulgent, because you've earned it. You worked hard for your money and probably scrimped along the way to pay for home improvements, vacations, college educations for your children, and the like. Retirement should provide the opportunity to pay yourself back— especially in ways that allow you to be involved in causes much bigger than yourself.

We've all heard stories about people who've retired from work and become cranky, bored, and restless within a few months. Sometimes they even return to the workaday lives they just left. These are the folks who failed to plan, and the folks for whom "I'm retired" is a euphemism for "I don't do anything anymore." These individuals weren't particularly introspective, didn't make intelligent and informed decisions, and certainly had no inspired game plan to lead the way.

The good news is that you can easily avoid that trap. Stop viewing retirement as a period of time, and start thinking about it as a lifestyle—a lifestyle of your own choosing. With a well-crafted Nest Egg Game Plan, you can turn avocations into new careers, add meaning to your life, give back to the community and the world at large, or reconnect with the dreams of your youth. People who believe that "youth is wasted on the young" never experienced the joy and excitement of an unencumbered and truly independent retirement. But that joy will not happen of itself—it's for you to create.

Our working years and retirement years do share something in common—we have to spend money to survive. In retirement, however, the decisions on how and where to spend your money are much more within your control. You can spend your money wisely to bring pleasure to yourself and others. With mortgage payments and tuition behind you, travel, continuing education, country club memberships, and spa weekends can all be part of your plan. Planned-gifting programs to your heirs or charities can also be considered, allowing you to witness the benefits of your generosity rather than waiting till you've passed. Retirement need not be a trap. Approach it as an opportunity and reap the benefits you've earned.

So how do you accomplish that? The answer differs from person to person but there is one common element: engagement. The most successful and satisfied retirees are physically engaged, mentally engaged, socially engaged, and community engaged. In a very real sense they approach their personal lives the same way they do their financial lives—that is, they build a diversified "personal portfolio" that provides satisfaction on many different but highly complementary levels. So just as your investment portfolio comprises different asset classes like stocks, bonds, and cash, your personal portfolio also comprises three different asset classes: your health and well-being, your interests and activities, and your involvement with people and the community.

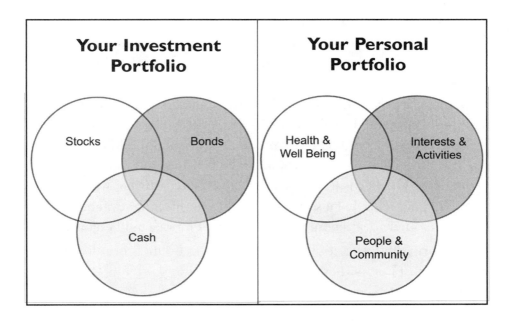

It's really quite a simple concept. Your investment portfolio is designed to deliver a lifetime income stream, and your personal portfolio is designed to provide a lifetime stream of contentment and fulfillment. Think of it as a "self-actualization" plan. The beautiful thing about retirement is that you can call the shots. You're no longer doing what someone else is telling you to do; you can do exactly what you want when you want to do it. But that doesn't happen by magic. You need to have a disciplined plan before and during retirement. Just as you begin building your investment portfolio by saving small amounts and watching the miracle of compounding create a sizeable nest egg, you build your personal portfolio one step at a time beginning when you're very young and continuing to the day you leave this life.

The retirees who live truly inspired lives have a breadth of interests and relationships. They engage in a variety of activities with a wide range of people. Going back to the investment portfolio analogy, the happiest retirees tend to be those who engage in "non-correlated" activities with "non-correlated" people. Examples of non-correlated activities would be cycling and gardening, golf and painting, or fishing and chess. The idea is that, if you're forced to give up one activity due to illness, injury, or some other reason, you'll still have other interests to keep your mind and body engaged. Examples of non-correlated people would be your spouse and your book club members, your fishing buddies and your college classmates, or your volunteer colleagues and your next-door neighbors. The key is to interact with and share your life with a broad group of people so that if someone leaves your life, an inevitable reality, you have other meaningful relationships to embrace and enjoy.

To bring this idea to life, let's look at three different retirees who are living inspired and engaged active lives.

Margo Chamberlain

When Margo Chamberlain turned 65 in 2008, she was already in her 10th year of retirement. After working for 13 years as a librarian in Massachusetts and New Mexico, followed by another 17 years as a human resources manager in the private sector, Margo retired in 1999 at the age of 55. It was every worker's dream. Leave the rat race at a young age and enjoy life to the fullest. In most people's dream scenario, however, they either won the lottery or received a hefty inheritance. In Margo's case, her dream came true by deciding she could live comfortably on about a third of her pre-retirement earnings.

Her income looked like this. She received a $500 monthly pension from her former employer, which netted about $200 after her healthcare premium was deducted. She had always contributed the maximum to her 401(k) plan and, due to the raging bull market of the 1980s and 1990s, it was worth $250,000 on the day she retired. She rolled her

401(k) into an IRA and, using the exception allowed in the IRS tax code [Section 72(t)] for "substantially equal periodic payments," she was able to take penalty-free withdrawals of $1,700 per month from her IRA. After 10 years' worth of withdrawals, Margo's IRA balance stood at $150,000 in January 2009.

When you do the math you'll see that Margo retired on an annual income of $26,400. The good news is that Margo had also done the math. Retiring was not a spur-of-the-moment decision. She had thought about it and planned it for years, so she knew exactly how much money would be coming in and where it would be going. The key component of her pre-retirement planning was to eliminate all debt. With discipline and purpose, she had been sending in a little extra with every mortgage payment and, as planned, she owned her home outright on the day she retired.

Margo's retirement income stream also worked exactly as planned, but she struggled a bit with other aspects of her retirement. Margo had always been a workaholic and she describes herself as being a "total mess" during the early days of retirement. "Despite having planned for it," Margo explained, "I was terrified that I would be confronted by long days and nights of doing nothing. And I had no idea what interested me."

One year after retiring, Margo was diagnosed with breast cancer. Shortly thereafter, in early 2001, she had a lumpectomy to remove the cancerous growth. She declined chemotherapy but did endure radiation treatments for about six weeks. Through the surgery and radiation treatments, Margo "experienced doing nothing for the very first time in my life—something that is truly anathema to a workaholic." She also *chose* to continue living. She was determined to heal and, indeed, has been cancer-free ever since.

Even before the cancer diagnosis, Margo began to enjoy the quiet time. She "learned to become interested and curious about everything" around her, and she was content to "lay low" until something caught her attention and inspired her to get actively involved. Always a spiritual person, Margo followed her interests and became an ordained minister of the "new thought" Church of Divine Science. She joyously embraced the opportunity to be a spiritual guide and began conducting wedding ceremonies and wedding vow renewals. Recently, Margo presided over her stepson's wedding, and she is now a delighted mother-in-law and grandmother.

Travel has always been the most important part of Margo's life, and that's where the biggest single slice of her income is directed. Over the last few years Margo has taken a three-month-long trip to France, where she attended art school; she visited Malta in 2006; and, in 2008, she spent a month in Argentina and Chile. The total cost of the 2008 trip was $4,000, and she never felt like she was skimping or missing any part of the experience.

Margo's most memorable and meaningful travel experience occurred in 2000, shortly after she retired, when she visited Ghana for a week. Margo was a "Global Investor" in "The Hunger Project" and was invited by the organization to tour the country as part of the African Woman Food Farmer Initiative. To quote from the organization's Website, "The Hunger Project firmly believes that empowering women to be key change agents is an essential element to achieving the end of hunger and poverty." That mission captured Margo's imagination and she pledged to contribute $5,000 a year to the organization. Keep in mind that $5,000 represented about 20 percent of her annual income. Margo's spirituality and giving-nature determined that the Hunger Project needed the money more than she did.

As Margo has aged, her income-generation strategy has evolved. She began collecting Social Security at age 62 and now receives $1,213 per month. She has also dabbled a bit in real estate, financed with a small inheritance from her mother and some home equity from her primary residence. She currently owns and rents two small one-family homes but, with the downturn in the housing market, the rent just barely covers her carrying costs. She also rents a mother-in-law apartment as well as a room in her home, netting about $900 a month.

Today, at the ripe young age of 65 and thanks to Robert Kiyosaki's advice in *Rich Dad Poor Dad,* Margo is creating multiple streams of income. Back in her working days, Margo had been very taken with the book *Your Money or Your Life: 9 Steps to Transforming Your Relationship with Money and Achieving Financial Independence.* She began hosting discussion groups at work to consider the issues raised by the book and subsequently created several workshops to address the fear most of us have about money. "My focus," Margo explains, was to "coach people into happy relationships with money." Today, Margo is focused on "teaching parents and grandparents how to teach kids about money," a springboard for the next entrepreneurial stage of Margo's life.

Terry McCue

Terry McCue is a retiree right out of central casting. She's a vivacious 87-year-old who's been married to the same man, Martin, for more than 60 years. She's the mother of six and the grandmother of 11. But none of those facts and figures get to the core of what makes Terry so special. Terry lives life to the fullest every day. And from her perspective, Terry never really retired; the years just flowed naturally from one to the next.

Terry is a classic example of a woman who came of age during the period of World War II. Following high school she attended art school and began working in the retail industry designing and building window displays. As World War II dragged on, she was recruited to work as a draftsman but found the work dreary and dull. After she and Martin married and began having children, Terry worked as a freelance graphic designer. She continued to design window displays but also worked on advertising campaigns and promotional flyers.

As good an artist as Terry was, it was her personality and people skills that really drove her success. People loved her enthusiasm, and it opened doors that would otherwise have been shut to what she describes as "a suburban housewife." One of her retail clients invited her to design a line of linens. Terry jumped at the challenge and created not one but six lines of dishtowels, bath towels, beach towels, and the like. And to top it off, she went ahead and also designed the packaging for the linens.

Right around the time most people officially retire, Terry began drawing pen-and-ink portraits of homes. Her work attracted the attention of a large local realty firm, she was invited in to make a presentation and display her work, and they hired her as their "artist of record" for homes they were representing for sale or purchase.

At that point, with her children grown and out of the office, Terry kicked her personal life into high gear. Somewhere between 65 and 70 she began taking tap-dancing lessons, an activity she continued until age 80. She performed for nursing homes, marched in a charity parade with 5,000 other dancers, and performed for the governor of New Jersey.

At age 68, she felt driven to go back to school and get an official college degree. She had received a certificate for attending art school back in the 1940s, but she wanted more. Terry enrolled in the art program at a local college, got some "life credits," and graduated with honors with her associate's degree.

One of Terry's daughters suffered with mental illness and that experience spurred her to get actively involved with a local support group for people with mentally ill children. As a result of her efforts, Terry was invited to serve on the board of directors of the New Jersey National Alliance on Mental Illness. She was excited about the position but humbled as well. Terry explains it like this: "There was little old me, a suburban housewife, surrounded by doctors, lawyers, and other professionals." She remained on the board for more than 25 years, with her tenure extending into retirement. Beginning in her 70s, Terry taught a "Journey of Hope" class to family members of mentally ill individuals, sharing her experiences and insight to help a new generation of parents, spouses, and siblings.

At age 79, Terry became a Eucharistic Minister of the Catholic Church, and to this day she delivers communion to parishioners who are in the hospital or unable to leave their homes. And at age 81, she joined the local art society and began painting "just for the joy of it."

Terry's *joie de vivre* directed her life and personal pursuits, but her consistent and conservative approach to money contributed strongly to her satisfying lifestyle. She and Martin never made a lot of money but, being products of the Great Depression, they always focused on making it go as far as possible. They helped finance their children's college education but never spent a lot on themselves. Once the kids were grown, however, Terry and Martin indulged their love of travel. Over the years they toured parts of Europe, the Caribbean, Mexico, Alaska, and most of the continental United States. They'd still be traveling today if Martin's physical condition allowed it.

The McCues own their own home and have no debt. Martin, who worked as a tollbooth collector for the New Jersey Parkway Commission, receives a state pension. They both receive Social Security benefits, which, along with monthly income from an annuity and interest from CDs, allow them to live comfortably and worry-free.

"It's interesting," explains Terry. "Money is less of a problem now than when we were younger."

That's probably because money was never a driving force in her life. She didn't let money issues overwhelm her during her working years, and she's not about to let it happen now.

James and Rosie Earl

James Earl was a young man of 56 when he lost his job. He and his wife of 35 years, Rosie, had to leave their big-city home and return to the rural farm town where they had grown up. The good news was that they didn't have to worry about money; the bad news was the work that had so defined their day-to-day lives was gone, and they weren't sure how best to replace it. As James describes it, they "awoke to an altogether new, unwanted, and potentially empty life." Rosie was more direct: She felt "angry, sad, anxious, and worried."

But rather than wallow in self-pity, the Earls took action. James had an unfulfilled lifelong ambition to teach, and he quickly secured a teaching position. He had always enjoyed woodworking and now had the time to build furniture or "to just bang on something" to clear his mind. Rosie became more introspective and set out to learn more about herself and her family. She spent hours talking with her mother and elderly aunts and uncles, as well as her siblings and childhood friends. The insights she gathered comforted her and paved the way for a whole new approach to living and interacting with the larger world.

As James and Rosie settled into their new life, they came to the realization that, as "retired people," they had a lot more leeway to chose their own path and establish their own priorities. Together they made the conscious and exciting decision that their future life did not need to be limited by their past experiences, and they decided to challenge themselves to think bigger and accomplish more.

Less than four years after beginning their forced retirement, the Earls began what would become a lifelong commitment to Habitat for Humanity, the nonprofit organization dedicated to eliminating homelessness and providing clean and comfortable shelter around the world. The Earls' first project was helping to renovate a dilapidated building on New York's Lower East Side and turning it into apartments for 19 needy families. Working alongside the future residents of the building, the Earls experienced an epiphany regarding the level of personal satisfaction that comes from knowing you truly are making a difference in someone's life. From that day forward, James and Rosie have volunteered with Habitat for Humanity for one week a year.

As part of their personal challenge to "think bigger," James and Rosie both got involved with organizations that had far-reaching aspirations. James joined an organization focused on resolving conflicts, protecting human rights, and preventing disease. As a result of the organization's efforts, worldwide cases of Guinea worm disease, which afflicted 3.5 million Africans in 1986, have been reduced by 99.7 percent and may be fully eradicated over the next few years.

For her part, Rosie has become a strong and active advocate for mental health and early childhood immunization. She is active in an organization dedicated to enhancing care-giving to the mentally ill and promoting positive change in the mental health field, and she volunteers for Project Interconnections, a nonprofit organization focused on providing housing for homeless people who are also mentally ill.

But don't think the Earls are "do-good workaholics." In addition to their charitable activities, the Earls take great delight in their four children, 11 grandchildren, and two great-grandchildren. James enjoys many active pursuits, including fly-fishing, woodworking, cycling, and tennis. Rosie too keeps physically active fly-fishing and biking with her husband, as well as enjoying swimming and bird-watching on her own.

The Earls' approach to retirement is characterized by their own words:

> ...the opportunities are boundless. No matter how much or how little we have accomplished in the first part of our lives, it is never too late for unprecedented experiences. The second half of our lives can actually be a time of greater risk-taking for those of us whose responsibilities may have left little room for taking chances before—not foolish or pointless risks, but risks that offer the hope of both real adventure and real reward, for ourselves and others. While some of our physical powers may be diminished, we have survival skills younger people may not have learned, a different kind of endurance that comes with the passage of time.

Those insights come from *Everything to Gain: Making the Most of the Rest of Your Life,* written by James Earl Carter and Rosalynn Carter, our former president and first lady. Regardless of how you feel about his presidency or political beliefs, Jimmy Carter has crafted a retirement of inspirational depth and reward. And Rosalynn, an educated and accomplished woman on her own prior to Jimmy's political career, has used retirement as an opportunity to build a reputation and lasting legacy separate and distinct from being the former president's wife.

And if you think that their retirement path was paved with glory because they once lived in the White House, consider that anyone can volunteer for Habitat for Humanity or Project Interconnections. Anyone can get involved with local or national organizations dedicated to health and education. Every community from rural Georgia to the streets of Manhattan offers opportunities to contribute and make a difference.

The only difference between Jimmy and Rosalynn and your retirement is that they committed and followed through on that commitment. You can do the same, if you choose.

Chapter 8

I NTELLIGENT:
Incorporating Best-Practice Decision-Making

A successful Nest Egg Game Plan depends on a seemingly never-ending series of decisions that continually test one's intelligence and fortitude. Tax considerations reign supreme in building an effective strategy, but they are not the only intellectual challenges you will face in retirement. Making the right choice regarding Social Security can have a significant impact on your retirement lifestyle. You also need to consider whether you are truly prepared to go it alone or if you'd be better off hiring a professional financial advisor to guide you. Part of that decision hinges on whether you have the emotional intelligence to systematically and unemotionally implement your game plan.

And keep in mind that the intelligence we're talking about in this chapter is quite different from IQ scores and advanced degrees. There are plenty of highly credentialed doctors, lawyers, engineers, and other educated types who are babes-in-the-woods when it comes to investing.

An intelligent Nest Egg Game Plan is not rocket science; it's more like a jigsaw puzzle. You've got all the pieces; you just need the time, inclination, and attention to detail to put them all together.

Tax-Smart Investing

Understanding the differing tax treatment of interest, dividends, and capital gains can earn you an extra 1 or 2 percent in after-tax investment returns over the course of a year. It's an easy and legal investment strategy that is all too often ignored by investors and advisors. Based on current tax regulations (which are always subject to change), dividends are taxed at a lower rate than interest, and long-term capital gains are taxed less than short-term gains. That means you can boost your earnings by strategically allocating tax-inefficient investments in your tax-deferred accounts (like IRAs and 401(k)s) and keep tax-efficient investments in your taxable accounts.

Here's why this is important. Dividends generated by corporate stock, and held in a taxable account, are taxed at 15 percent. However, those exact same dividends generated in a tax-deferred account will be taxed at ordinary income rates when withdrawn, which, for the vast majority of middle-income Americans, will be significantly higher than 15 percent. As an example, if you assume a 28-percent marginal tax rate, then $1,000 worth of dividends would deliver net proceeds of $850 in a taxable account versus $720 when withdrawn from a tax-deferred account.

Similarly, if you're going to engage in short-term trading strategies or own mutual funds with high turnover rates, you're likely to generate a lot of short-term capital gains that are taxed as ordinary income and, as a result, would be better suited to your tax-deferred accounts. You'll still have to pay ordinary income tax when the gains are withdrawn, but by deferring the tax liability you get to enjoy the miracle of compounding on the full amount of your gains.

Tax-efficient investments include:

▷   Dividend-paying stocks.

▷   Many exchange traded funds (ETFs) and index funds (due to the low turnover rates).

▷   Municipal bonds and municipal bond funds.

▷   Tax-managed mutual funds (though the performance record of these are somewhat spotty, due in part to higher management fees).

▷   Treasuries if you live in a place like New York or California with a high state income tax.

Tax-inefficient investments include:

▷   Active mutual funds with high turnover rates.

▷   TIPS (Treasury-Inflation Protected Securities).

▷   REITs. In most cases, the dividends generated by Real Estate Investment Trusts are treated as ordinary income.

▷   Interest from corporate bonds and bond funds, bank CDs, and money market funds.

▷   Zero-coupon bonds.

Mutual fund investors need to pay close attention to two other considerations. By law mutual funds have to distribute realized gains to their shareholders. This typically happens towards the end of the calendar year. The problem is that investors who purchase the fund shortly before the distribution will be taxed on a gain they never received. Here's an example of how this could happen. An investor buys 1,000 shares of the ABC Growth Fund at $10 on November 15th. On December 15th, the fund is still at $10, but ABC Investments declares a distribution equal to 5 percent of the fund's net asset value. If you chose to take distributions in cash, you'll receive a check for $500 and you'll have 1,000 shares priced at $9.50. If you chose to reinvest distributions, you'll now have 1,052.63 shares priced at $9.50. In either case you'll still have $10,000, but you will also owe federal and state income tax on the $500 phantom gain. There is no logic to this methodology, and several congressional attempts have been made to change the law, but it remains on the books. So, please *do not* invest money in a mutual fund in a taxable account between October 1st and December 31st unless the fund has already declared and paid its annual distribution.

The second related issue for mutual fund shareholders involves "embedded gains" in mutual funds. Remember that in the previous paragraph we said that mutual funds had to distribute *realized* gains to shareholders. A realized gain means a security has been sold for a profit. An unrealized gain refers to a security that is still being held in the mutual fund's portfolio that is worth more than its purchase price. When the security is sold, the gain will be realized and the shareholders at the time of the distribution will be taxed on the gain, regardless of whether they were invested in the fund when the security was originally purchased and whether they benefited from the increase in price. This represents a significant issue for mutual fund investors, but, unfortunately, there is no easy way to gather this information. Services like Morningstar are hit-or-miss in providing this level of detail in their "tax analysis" review of individual funds, so your best bet would be to call the mutual fund company directly and ask for the specific fund's potential exposure to embedded gains. They should be able to provide this information; if they can't, you may want to consider a different fund company.

Tax-Smart Income Generation

The general guideline is to spend down your taxable accounts during the early years of retirement and let your tax-deferred savings grow for as long as possible. Indeed that is the best approach for most people, but with two caveats.

First, if you believe your tax rate will be higher in the future, it could be advantageous to draw down your tax-deferred savings earlier rather than later. Most people assume they will be in a lower tax bracket as they get older and, if the tax rates remain as they are today, that will probably be true. Keep in mind, however, that marginal tax rates are at a historic low. Income tax rates have declined dramatically over the last 20 years, and that causes us to forget that, in the not-so-distant past, the top marginal tax rate was 70 percent. The next 20 years are likely to be quite different from the last 20. The global economic crisis has prompted a huge stimulus package from the U.S. government, and our national debt is measured in the trillions of dollars. It is not inconceivable to think that tax hikes may be one tool in paying down that debt. If that were to be the case, then allowing your tax-deferred accounts to grow could push you into a higher tax bracket just when you least expect it and when you can least afford it.

The second scenario that would prompt you to withdraw from tax-deferred accounts before taxable accounts applies to people with large tax-deferred balances. That's because of the impact of required minimum distributions (RMDs). The RMD is the IRS-mandated amount of money you must withdraw from your qualified accounts once you hit age 70.5. The initial RMD must be made by April 1st of the year following the year you turn 70.5. Subsequent RMDs must be taken each calendar year. Your RMD is recalculated annually based on age and life expectancy (as well as the age and life expectancy of your spouse or other beneficiary). As the individual gets older, the increases in the RMD become sharply higher (due to a shorter life expectancy). Individuals with tax-deferred balances of $1 million, who wait until 70.5 to begin withdrawals, could see RMDs increase to the $100,000 range when they reach their early 80s and double that if they live to age 90. In addition to being exceptionally fortunate, individuals who find themselves in this situation are well advised to begin withdrawing from their tax-deferred accounts and allowing their taxable accounts to grow. Although there is no hard rule on who should tap their tax-deferred accounts earlier than age 70.5, it generally applies to people whose IRA balances exceed their lifetime spending needs. Other factors include anticipated longevity, rates of return, and future tax rates.

Now here's some good news. None of this applies to Roth IRAs. Future tax rates have no impact on Roths and there are no RMDs for Roth IRAs. Withdrawals are always tax-free, and you can let your account grow untouched forever.

One other tax-smart consideration involves distributions from mutual funds. During your wealth-accumulation years, it made sense to automatically reinvest dividends, interest, and capital gains distributions from mutual funds. Doing so was a type of dollar-cost averaging and allowed you to buy more shares that would generate more distributions and further accelerate the miracle of long-term compounding. During retirement, however, automatic reinvesting is the wrong choice for two reasons:

1. By allocating these types of distributions to your cash account, you'll be able to use these funds as an income source without having to sell other positions and incurring additional tax liabilities.

2. Because different asset classes generate differing levels of distributions (for example, a high-yield bond fund throws off a lot more interest than a short-term bond fund), allocating distributions to a cash account will make it easier to maintain the correct balance within your asset allocation strategy.

The Smart Approach to Social Security

The Social Security Administration (SSA) reports that the most common question they receive from constituents is "What is the best age to start receiving retirement benefits?" Our response would be identical to the one posted on the SSA's Website: "There is no one 'best age' for everyone and, ultimately, it is your choice."

You have three options on when to begin collecting Social Security:

> **Before "Full Retirement Age" (FRA):** Although FRA varies depending on when you were born (as shown in the table that follows), anyone can start receiving benefits as early as age 62. Doing so, however, will reduce your monthly benefit by 25 percent to 30 percent.

> **At FRA:** The Social Security Administration will calculate your monthly benefit based on your average earnings over 35 years, with a maximum earnings cap of $106,800 for 2009 and a maximum monthly benefit of $2,323.

> **After FRA:** Each year you choose to defer receiving Social Security benefits, your monthly benefit increases by about 8 percent, as the accompanying graph shows. Keep in mind, however, that you must begin drawing benefits at age 70.

Full Retirement Age vs. Benefit at Age 62 (assuming $1,000 monthly benefit at full retirement age)		
Year of Birth	**Full Retirement Age**	**Benefit at Age 62**
1943–1954	66	$750
1955	66 and 2 months	$741
1956	66 and 4 months	$733
1957	66 and 6 months	$725
1958	66 and 8 months	$716
1959	66 and 10 months	$708
1960 or later	67	$700

From the federal government's perspective, it doesn't matter when you choose to receive Social Security. The cost to the SSA will be same (or is expected to be the same) whether you start at age 62 or age 70. That's because the actuarial computations that determine benefit amounts are designed to pay out the same lifetime benefit regardless of when you start. Here's a simple way to think about it. Let's assume the SSA's actuarial table predicts that the average person of your age will die at age 80 and your monthly benefit at age 62 equals $750 a month, or $9,000 a year. If you retire at age 62, you will have collected $162,000 by age 80. If you retire at age 70, and the same mortality expectation is used, you would receive a monthly benefit of $1,320 (or $15,840 a year) with total payments of $158,400 by age 80. Eighteen years worth of $750 monthly payments equals roughly the same as ten years of $1,320 monthly payments. To the federal government it's a numbers game relying on the law of averages.

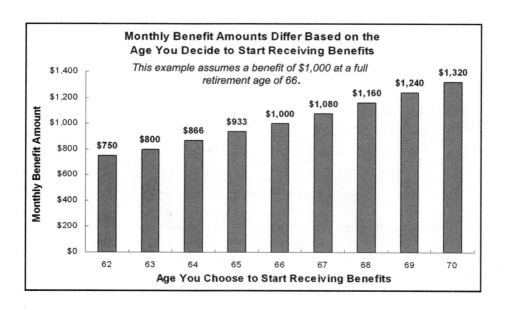

Of course "averages" tend to be meaningless in real life, especially in a world where one in four 65-year-olds will live past age 90, and one in 10 of them will live past 95. For most people, the decision on when to begin Social Security depends on a wide range of factors, including one's health, longevity of family members, other sources of retirement income, plans to work in retirement, and financial needs (both immediate and anticipated).

As we stated at the beginning of this section, there is no magic age at which to begin receiving Social Security benefits. Nonetheless, we feel compelled to offer some guidelines to assist in the decision-making process. So here are some basic dos and don'ts:

> ▷ Do not take Social Security benefits before your full retirement age if you are still working and earn more than $14,160 (the limit for 2009). Your benefit payments will be reduced by $1 for every $2 you earn above the limit. (This isn't as bad as it sounds because, in true federal taxation fashion, the full story is a little more complicated. If the SSA does reduce your benefit because of earned income, it will then recalculate your benefit amount when you reach full retirement age to reflect those withholdings, and your monthly benefit will be increased.)

> ▷ Do not defer taking Social Security beyond your full retirement age just because you're still working. Your benefits will not be reduced by your earnings; however, your Social Security benefits will be subject to federal income taxes. If you file as an "individual," Social Security benefits will be taxable if your total income is more than $25,000. If you file a joint return, Social Security benefits will be taxable if you and your spouse have a total income of more than $32,000.

▷ Do continue to work until full retirement age if your earned income took a big jump in recent years. The SSA calculates your benefit based on your average earnings over 35 years, so it's possible that an extra two or three years of working can appreciably increase your FRA benefit.

▷ Do consider the impact of your decision on your family. In the case of a married couple, it usually makes sense for the spouse with the higher earnings record to wait until full retirement age. This will ensure that the surviving spouse would receive the full benefits if the higher-earning spouse were to die first.

▷ Do not begin receiving Social Security benefits at age 62 in order to help pay your living expenses. This would constitute a band-aid approach to a serious financial problem and will only serve to worsen your financial situation as you get older. In general, the larger the role Social Security will play in financing your retirement, the longer you should wait to begin payments.

▷ Do give serious consideration to your health and your family's medical history. In many respects, choosing to take Social Security at age 62 versus age 66 or age 70 is a bet on how long you're going to live. But like all bets, try to have the odds stacked in your favor by considering as much information as possible.

The following three graphs depict the breakeven points and aggregate payout amounts when starting Social Security benefits at age 62 versus age 66, age 62 versus age 70, and age 66 versus age 70. The numbers are striking and reinforce the need to make this decision carefully and with considerable forethought.

For most people, the major decision is whether to begin Social Security payments at age 62 or wait until age 66. In this example, the breakeven point—or the point in time when your accumulated payments beginning at age 66 equal and begin to surpass the accumulated payments you've received since age 62—occurs roughly at age 75. Should you live to be 100 years old, your lifetime benefits would be increased by $166,000 by deferring Social Security for four years. If you die prior to age 75, you might have scrimped unnecessarily in your early years of retirement.

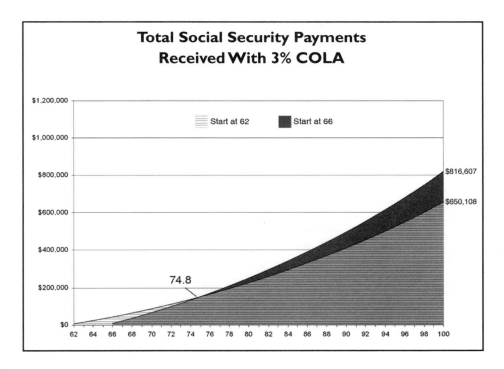

This next illustration compares deferring Social Security payments to age 70 rather than age 62. The lifetime payout to age 100 totals $350,000 more if you wait to age 70.

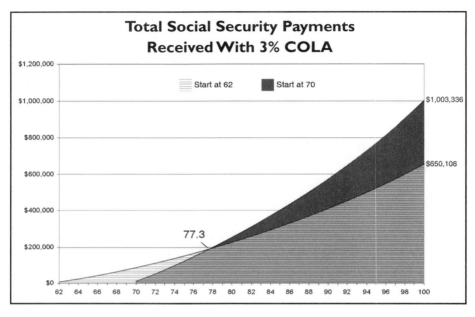

The final illustration compares starting Social Security at age 66 versus age 70. The breakeven point is age 79 with an extra $185,000 of lifetime payments.

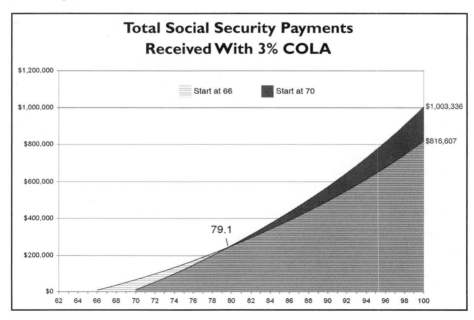

Social Security's COLA Is the Real Thing

Inflation is the mortal enemy of retirees, but Social Security has a built-in inflation fighter: the annual cost-of-living-adjustment (COLA). Because these COLA increases tend to be small—usually between 2 and 4 percent—they are often ignored by retirees and their advisors, but they can play a huge role in ensuring the success of your Nest Egg Plan. Indeed, someone who retired 20 or 30 years ago is likely collecting COLA benefits that exceed his or her original benefit. Similarly, someone who retired in 2008 with the maximum full retirement age benefit of $2,185 per month would collect more than $1.2 million in benefits after 30 years, assuming (as the Social Security Administration does) a 2.8-percent COLA. That is serious money by any measure.

For many retirees, Social Security is the only element of their income stream that does adjust upward to match inflation. For individuals in good health with a family history of longevity, a strong argument can be made for delaying Social Security to age 66 or 70 to further strengthen the inflation-fighting power of the COLA benefit. The compounding effects of COLA cannot be stressed enough in world where a 65-year-old couple has a 40-percent chance that one of them will live to age 90 or beyond.

The best way to think about Social Security is as an inflation-protected immediate fixed annuity—backed by the full faith and credit of the U.S. government. It would not be unusual for a working couple to retire with combined Social Security benefits of $25,000 to $40,000 per year. In order to generate that kind of income, coupled with annual increases to match inflation, you would need a retirement nest egg of $600,000 to $1 million, assuming a 4-percent withdrawal rate, to properly fund your retirement years. So, going back to Chapter 2, make sure you factor in Social Security when you calculate your "number." Doing so may ease a lot of your anxiety.

Social Security: Get It While You Can?

One factor that drives many retirees to begin collecting Social Security on their very first day of eligibility is the fear that the federal government will abolish, phase out, or otherwise modify the program. Skepticism about the future of Social Security can best be exemplified by the widespread, albeit apocryphal, survey results showing that more Generation Xers believe in aliens than believe they will ever collect a penny of Social Security. Even the trustees of the Social Security program candidly admit that something needs to be done, as this direct quote from the Social Security Administration Website attests:

> Social Security is not sustainable at currently scheduled levels over the long term with current tax rates without large infusions of additional revenue. There will be a growing shortfall once the trust fund reserves are exhausted in 2041.... If Social Security is not changed, then by about 2041 payroll taxes will have to be increased, the benefits of today's younger workers will have to be cut, or some other source of revenue, like transfers from general revenues, will be required.

Many elements of constructing a retirement income stream can and should inspire angst, but we don't believe Social Security should be included in that category—at least not for people who are nearing retirement age. Though there are no guarantees in life, we believe Social Security will be there in its current form for people born before 1955 and in a modified form for those who are younger. Keep in mind that Social Security has evolved through the years. In 1983, legislation was passed to gradually raise the full retirement age from 65 to 67 beginning in 2000. This was done partly in recognition of the substantially increased life spans and more active lifestyles of the current adult generation, and partly to responds to concerns about the program's long-term solvency. Future evolution of the program is likely to follow a similar methodology of extending full retirement age, increasing the payroll tax, or reducing benefits for wealthy retirees.

Emotional Intelligence

As intelligently designed as your Nest Egg Game Plan may be, its success depends in large part on your own level of *emotional intelligence*. During the last few years behavioral finance has become a hot topic of discussion, and the market meltdown of 2008 has drawn even greater attention to the psychology of investing. It's long been known that individual investors tend to lag the market, and that shortfall usually results from fear, greed, over-confidence, and a fixation on the rearview mirror.

Let's begin with the latter—our fixation on the past, especially the immediate past—because that drives most of our investing mistakes. The table on page 128 shows how two sample portfolios perform over a three-year period. Based on the annual returns, the two portfolios have markedly different risk-reward characteristics. Although Portfolio A provides a consistent 10-percent return, Portfolio B delivers returns ranging from +22 percent to –10 percent. After the three-year period, however, both portfolios deliver similar aggregate performance. The key point of this table is presented in the bottom row. In the first year, our own "Joe the Investor" put his money in Portfolio A. When the first year ended, he saw that Portfolio B did much better, so he switched his investment to Portfolio B. In the second year, however, Portfolio A outperformed Portfolio B, so Joe switched his money back to Portfolio A for the third year. Joe's obsession with the past and chasing last year's winners caused him to greatly under-perform both portfolios and end up with a total return that would barely keep pace with inflation.

Though this is an exaggerated example, it points out the primary folly of individual investors who buy the hottest 5-star mutual funds and then watch in sad disbelief as they plummet to the ground in flames. Do yourself a huge favor and eliminate this tendency to chase performance by trading in and out of investments. Instead, as Warren Buffett's advised, "Only buy something that you'd be perfectly happy to hold if the market shut down for 10 years" and take to heart his reminder that "the investor of today does not profit from yesterday's growth."

$100,000 Initial Investment				
	Year 1	Year 2	Year 3	Ending Account Value
Portfolio A	+10%	+10%	+10%	$133,100
Portfolio B	+22%	−10%	+21%	$132,858
Portfolio Chasing	+10%	−10%	+10%	$108,900
(Switching between Portfolio A and Portfolio B based on the best performance in the PRIOR year)	Portfolio A chosen at the start of Year 1	Portfolio B chosen based on performance in Year 1	Portfolio A chosen based on performance in Year 2	

Emotional intelligence, or lack thereof, also inspires overconfidence among many investors. People, being people, have a tendency to greatly overestimate their knowledge of and their ability to do just about everything. This tendency is so prevalent that it even has a name—the Lake Wobegon Effect—after the idyllic town of handsome men, strong women, and precocious children that Garrison Keillor made famous on his *Prairie Home Companion* radio series. Investors manifest the Lake Wobegon Effect by believing they can outperform the market. This sense of overconfidence is especially present during bull markets when individuals become increasingly aggressive as the bubble gets closer to bursting. Investors also suffer from "hindsight bias," remembering their good decisions while overlooking their poor ones, and they often have a hard time distinguishing between lucky decisions and intelligently thought-out decisions.

The flipside of overconfidence is fear. When the market is moving down, investors' overconfidence often prompts them to initially view it as a "buying opportunity." However, once the downward trend continues for a prolonged period of time, most investors either get paralyzed with fear (that is, fear of making the wrong decision) or they dump everything and move to cash (usually just before the market bottoms).

And then we have greed. There's a Wall Street saying that "bulls make money, bears make money, but pigs gets slaughtered." Greed manifests itself by the frenetic (and often random) buying and selling of equity positions and the continual monitoring of CNBC and Bloomberg TV to see what the "smart money" is doing. Though somewhat counterintuitive, greed is also responsible for the "disposition effect" or the reluctance of investors to realize capital losses. Investors tend to sell their winners too soon to lock in profits but are unwilling to sell their losers in the hope that the stock will rebound and they can get back to even.

The best-laid Nest Egg Game Plan can be thwarted by emotionally inspired errors of judgment, but you can thwart emotional missteps by following a few simple guidelines:

> ▷ Establish a disciplined approach to buying and selling, and put it in writing. Use stop-loss orders to automatically sell a holding that declines by more than 10 percent, and re-evaluate every holding that increases by 10 percent to ensure that the reasons why you bought it still hold true.

> ▷ Accept the fact that the market will sometimes go down, sometimes for long periods. Ensure that your strategy considers worst-case scenarios and is not dependent on a steady string of double-digit increases in the stock market.

- ⊳ Automatically rebalance your portfolio using a rules-based methodology (for example, whenever a holding moves above or below a certain price point or exceeds a predetermined percentage of your overall portfolio). This will force you to buy low and sell high.

- ⊳ Don't act in haste. If a particular investment is a wise choice today, it'll be a wise choice tomorrow.

- ⊳ The bottom line: Don't let your emotions cloud, confuse, or control your investment decisions.

Be Smart About Getting Advice

One of the most important decisions you need to make when designing your Nest Egg Game Plan is whether you can do it yourself or whether you should hire a financial advisor. As we stated earlier in this chapter, investing is not rocket science, but it does require time and a level of knowledge and commitment that may exceed your abilities and interest. If so, then an advisor is probably a good choice—but please choose wisely.

Financial advisors come in two main varieties. The first and most common variety work for broker-dealers like Merrill Lynch, Smith Barney, or scores of smaller investment firms affiliated with banks and insurance companies. These brokers tend to be compensated by commissions generated by the products they sell to their clients. Brokers are regulated by the Financial Industry Regulatory Authority (more commonly known as FINRA). FINRA, which is funded by the very brokerage firms it regulates, requires that brokers only recommend products that are "suitable" for their clients. The other type of financial advisor is a Registered Investment Advisor, or RIA. The Securities and Exchange Commission (SEC) regulates RIAs and requires that they serve in a fiduciary capacity for their clients—in other words, they must focus on recommendations that are in the clients' best interests. RIAs do not receive commissions; instead they are compensated directly by their clients, usually in the form of an agreed-upon flat fee or a fee based on assets under management.

The two key words in the preceding paragraph are *suitable* and *fiduciary,* and you need to understand the difference and determine which is better for you. Here's a simple way to think about it. Let's say you're a client who needs some exposure to the S&P 500. You don't believe in active management and want a simple index fund benchmarked to the S&P 500. A broker is likely to offer you an index fund, often managed by his own firm, that pays an upfront commission and/or annual trail commissions. In order to pay those commissions, the fund has to boost its expenses—thereby reducing the return you get on your investment. Nonetheless, it is a suitable investment, and the broker is under no obligation to inform you that there are less-expensive alternatives or that his actions may represent a conflict of interest. An RIA, on the other hand, would have a fiduciary obligation to recommend a low-cost index fund or ETF. Doing otherwise would be grounds to lose his or her license.

In addition to the issues of suitability, fiduciary responsibility, and cost, you also should consider personal dynamics. You'll be entrusting a lot of responsibility to your advisor, so spend enough time up front in the interview process to make sure you feel trust, confidence, and a personal connection.

Referrals and recommendations from friends, family, and coworkers are among the best ways to find a qualified advisor. Do your homework, and don't feel rushed to make a decision. And if the potential advisor says anything about guarantees, too-good-to-be-true performance numbers, or immediately begins making product recommendations, cross him or her off your list. You want to be advised, not sold.

Chapter 9

INTELLIGIBLE:
Writing It Down and Keeping It Up

Men and women, college grads and high school dropouts, rich dads and poor dads, young people and old—almost all of them share one thing in common: They have no idea what they're invested in and would be unable to describe their investment strategy. If you were to ask the typical investor to list the holdings in his 401(k) plan, he is far more likely to say, "I'm in Fidelity" or "I'm with Vanguard" rather than naming a particular fund or describing a specific asset class. That laissez-faire attitude has a severely limiting effect during one's accumulation years, but it can spell disaster during retirement when there is very little time to recover from missteps.

The best way to ensure that you fully understand your Nest Egg Game Plan, unequivocally buy into it, and are able to successfully implement it is to follow the advice of the great football strategist Vince Lombardi, who advocated "planning your work and working your plan."

That means you have to put Your Nest Egg Game Plan in writing via a personalized Investment Policy Statement (IPS). The process of documenting your plan makes it more real, places the responsibility for achieving it firmly in your lap, and creates a disciplined approach to your investing activity. Your IPS needs to be written and organized in a manner that is understandable by spouses, children, parents, and any other interested parties—because if *they* can understand it, that means *you* truly understand it as well.

Investment Policy Statements have traditionally been used by corporations, endowments, and institutions to oversee and monitor the management of their investment portfolios. They're also fairly common for affluent individuals who work with private wealth managers. Unfortunately, they are rarely created for individual investors of moderate means, and their absence is a key factor in why most investors do not know what they own or why they own it. We believe an IPS is a requisite for all investors, but especially for investors who choose to manage their portfolios on their own.

A well-constructed IPS will spell out your investment goals and articulate the game plan and strategy to achieve those goals. A key benefit of an IPS is that it creates a systematic approach to money management that removes emotion—or at least most of it—from the investing equation. That systematic, unemotional approach helps maintain focus on the long-term during periods of extreme market fluctuations when it's most tempting to jump ship. Investment Policy Statements typically include a statement of overall investment philosophy and address issues such as risk tolerance levels, asset allocation strategy, rebalancing methodology, diversification techniques, and security selection. Other IPS considerations may include tax planning, gifting, philanthropic goals, and wealth transfer. Procedures for monitoring the plan are also specified.

Like all aspects of life, however, your IPS is not carved in stone. Instead, you should view it as a living document. It presents a long-term, over-arching game plan, but it needs to be flexible enough to respond to changing personal needs (for example, health issues) and external factors (unexpectedly high or low stock-market performance and interest rates). You'll need to review your IPS annually to ensure it is still on target.

Your IPS: An Annual Wealth Care Check-Up

Perhaps the best way to think about your IPS is to consider a medical analogy. Whereas every other aspect of your Nest Egg Game Plan involves an "exam" and a "diagnosis," the IPS focuses on the cure: the "prescription" and the periodic follow-up to ensure that your "treatment" is still working. Your IPS details what you learned during the exam and diagnosis stages and then translates that into an actionable plan. It turns your strategy and tactical approach into reality. Most importantly, it helps you continually assess how well your income-producing and asset-protecting actions are performing and measure how well the results are aligned with your long-term plan. By doing this on a regular basis, you can realign your actions before the issue or problem becomes a crisis that threatens your long-term security.

The Investment Policy Statement for a pension plan or endowment is typically created and signed by an oversight committee. Continuing the medical analogy, this committee serves as the plan's "physician" and is held accountable for the success or failure of the treatment. In the case of your Nest Egg Game Plan IPS, unless you're working with a financial advisor, you will serve as both the patient and physician. Without repeating the pros and cons of hiring an investment advisor, this self-diagnosing and self-policing approach clearly has some serious drawbacks—but they are drawbacks that, if understood and accounted for, can be moderated if not totally eliminated. The key success factors are:

- ▹ Understanding your goals.

- ▹ Establishing clear and quantifiable expectations.

- ▹ Ensuring those goals and expectations are realistic. (For example, planning to withdraw 10 percent of your portfolio annually or earning a 10-percent after-tax return on your investments is neither smart nor sustainable.)

- ▹ Holding yourself truly accountable. If the plan is not working after a year or two, promise yourself to get expert assistance.

As the first step in holding yourself accountable, we strongly suggest that you sign and date your personal IPS. If it's a joint IPS, both parties should sign and date. As silly as this may feel, it has a strong psychological impact that will go a long way to ensuring your success.

Your IPS Fact-Finder

Before putting pen to paper, or whatever the digital equivalent analogy would be, spend some time gathering all the relevant information about your current and anticipated financial situation. Use these questions to jump-start the process:

- ▹ How much is your investment portfolio worth today?

- ▹ If you own a home, how much equity do you have?

- ▹ What are your liabilities (home mortgage, auto loans, credit card balances, and tax obligations)?

- ▹ Do you have any other sources of income or capital appreciation (such as Social Security, a company pension plan, cash-value life insurance, rental property, or precious metals)?

- ▹ What are your current expenses (including everything from groceries to medical insurance to utilities to vacations)? Will these expenses likely go up, go down, or remain the same over the foreseeable future?

> In today's dollars, how much annual income do you require to be comfortable?

> How much liquid cash do you need to have access to?

> What are your expectations for the stock market, bonds, and inflation?

> How much risk—or fluctuation in account value—are you willing to accept? How will you define and manage risk within your portfolio?

> Do you truly have the ability, desire, and fortitude to manage your investment portfolio on your own, or would you benefit from professional assistance?

> How will you monitor the performance of your portfolio as compared to the broader market?

> Are you adequately insured?

> Do you have a will or other estate plan?

> How long would you expect to live? What happens to Your Nest Egg Game Plan if you live five or 10 years longer than you expect?

Writing Your Investment Policy Statement

To revisit the medical analogy one final time, many physicians persist in using Latin when writing patient prescriptions. This tradition began centuries ago when Latin was viewed as a universal language that, because it was a dead language no longer in daily use, was less subject to misinterpretation. Today, Latin prescriptions are the last vestige of the cloak of secrecy and self-importance that once surrounded the medical profession. When writing your personal IPS, use plain language that is free of jargon and easily understandable. You are communicating with yourself, so there is no need for long-winded flowery statements of philosophy or highly subjective meanderings. Stick to the facts and figures, and you'll be better able to stick to the plan and make it succeed.

NOTE: The sample IPS that follows is available on our Website, www.NestEggGamePlan.com, as a free MS Word document that you can download, edit, and personalize.

Sample
Nest Egg Game Plan IPS

Profile

John is 67 years old and Jane is 64 years old. We are married with three grown children. We own a home worth approximately $500K with a $900 monthly mortgage payment. We expect to have the mortgage paid off in three years. While we currently plan to remain in our home during the first five to 10 years of retirement, we are exploring opportunities to relocate—thereby freeing up some of our home equity value. If and when we choose to relocate, we will substantially revise this IPS to reflect our changed situation.

John retired two years ago and has been working part-time, earning about $10,000 per year. When Jane retires next year, John will stop working and we will begin our "official" retirement. At that time, we will both begin collecting Social Security.

Neither of us will receive a corporate pension, but we have been good savers during our working lives and believe we have accumulated a comfortable nest egg. When John retired, he rolled over his 401(k) into an IRA that is currently worth $220,000. Jane has continued to contribute to her company's 401(k) and her account totals about $105,000. We have a joint brokerage account with another $180,000 in mutual funds, stocks, and bonds, as well as savings accounts and CDs worth $75,000. In addition, Jane owns a one-third share of a vacation home with her siblings (with her share worth approximately $140,000).

The approximate value of our investable assets, as of the initial signing of this IPS, is $580,000 allocated among several accounts as summarized below:

Joint brokerage account	$180,000
Savings and CDs	$75,000
Jane's 401(k)	$105,000
John's IRA	$220,000

Between now and her retirement, Jane will contribute an additional $6,000 to her 401(k).

Expectations and Goals

Our over-arching goal is to generate $50,000 of annual income, in today's dollars, during our first year of retirement and to have that amount increase by a 3% inflationary factor in each subsequent year. We plan to meet that goal by withdrawing 4% from our investment account (approximately $23,000) to supplement our Social Security payments ($17,000 for John and $11,000 for Jane).

We are at a point in our financial lives where we are not concerned about "beating the market." Rather than taking on the additional risk necessary to truly and consistently beat the market—ignoring the fact that neither of us believe it's even possible to do so—we are focused on generating consistent returns that satisfy our income needs. Having said that, however, we do not believe that the stock market will deliver the double-digit returns we enjoyed in the 1990s, and we will aim for a more realistic average annual return of 6%.

We love our kids and grandchildren and would love to be able to leave them an inheritance, but doing so is not a priority and will not determine the success or failure of our Nest Egg Pension Plan. Our will specifies our wishes regarding the distribution of our estate should we both leave this world.

Asset-Allocation Strategy

The following table shows the asset allocation targets we have established for our overall portfolio. Because we are managing this allocation strategy across multiple accounts—rather than ensuring each individual account includes this specific asset breakdown—it is acceptable that some individual accounts will be more concentrated in certain assets than others.

Asset Class	Target Allocation
Cash Equivalents: Money-Market Funds, CD's, and Short-Term Bonds	10%
U.S. Government Bonds Corporate Bonds	30%
U.S. Treasury Inflation-Protected Bonds	10%
International Bonds	10%
U.S Large Company Stock	5%
U.S. Mid-Sized Company Stock	5%
U.S. Small Company Stock	5%
International Stock (Developed and Emerging)	10%
Real Estate (REITs)	5%
Commodities and Natural Resources	10%

This approach allows us to minimize transaction costs and more easily and efficiently monitor performance and allocation percentages.

Due to the current low interest rate environment, the focus of our fixed income holdings will be short-term durations (six to 24 months). We do not want to tie up our money in long-term fixed income instruments that will likely be unable to match future inflation rates. In addition, due to current stock market volatility and historically high yields for many blue-chip stocks, we will reduce some of our exposure to the broader markets and focus on a smaller number of holdings of individual securities as well as dividend-focused index funds and ETFs.

Investment Methodology

We believe strongly that lower expense investment options will provide more effective exposure to the broader market. As a result, we will invest primarily in no-load index funds and exchange-traded funds. We will complement these core holdings with a small allocation to active management in select asset classes like real estate and high-yield bonds.

In addition to our core mutual fund and ETF holdings, we will select and hold a small number of individual U.S. stocks. Our selection criteria requires that these stocks be rated either "A" or "B" by Charles Schwab, have a price-earnings ratio lower than the S&P 500, and have a dividend yield higher than the S&P 500.

We will also invest in individual bonds and CDs, using a laddered approach to support our cash flow needs and respond to current interest rate fluctuations.

While we very much believe in the value of a guaranteed, immediate fixed-rate annuity, we have made the decision that current rates are too low to lock in for the rest of our lives. We will monitor annuity interest rates and payouts on an ongoing basis, and we would expect to invest 25% of our investment portfolio in a guaranteed income product sometime over the next three to five years.

Income Generation Strategy

In order to somewhat insulate ourselves from the ups and downs of the stock market, we will create a separate "daily expenses account" to fund our day-to-day living expenses. This account will be funded with $50,000 and will be invested in money market accounts and short-term (six months or less) CDs. This is equivalent to approximately two years' worth of income needs and will help ensure that we don't have to sell assets at fire-sale prices during periods of market declines.

All dividends, interest payments, and capital gain distributions will be paid in cash, rather than being reinvested, and will be used to replenish the daily expenses account.

In order to keep our tax burden as low as possible—and maximize the benefits of tax-deferral—we will strive to withdraw funds from our taxable accounts before tapping our IRAs, or at least until the minimum required distributions kick in.

Monitoring Process

Our asset-allocation model will be reviewed and maintained using a rules-based rebalancing methodology. Rather than rebalancing on a calendar basis—for example, quarterly or annually—each asset class is assigned a percentage threshold that determines when rebalancing occurs. For example, if the recommended allocation to Asset X is 10%, the thresholds might be set at 8% and 12%. If the proportional value of Asset X rises above or falls below those thresholds, the asset will be rebalanced back to the original allocation.

This rebalancing process will take into account the transaction costs and tax implications of buying or selling a given security. Whenever possible, this rebalancing process will use current cash flow from interest and dividends to keep the respective allocations aligned with the overall strategy. In addition, we will further strive to keep our asset allocation strategy in balance by withdrawing money from those investment vehicles that have outperformed and, as a result, represent a larger-than-desired percentage of the overall portfolio.

In addition to rebalancing, we will evaluate the results of our overall portfolio against the broad market on a semi-annual basis. In addition, we will compare the results generated by each asset class against its Morningstar peer group—for example, our large-cap stock investments will be compared against similar large-cap mutual funds and ETFs. While we do not expect to change investment options regularly, if we see a longer-term trend of below-average performance we will consider making a change.

I/We understand and agree with this Investment Policy Statement:

X _____   _____

John Doe   Date

X _____   _____

Jane Doe   Date

Chapter 10

I NFORMED:
Separating Fact From Fiction

The financial markets seem to suffer from severe multiple personality disorder. Irrational exuberance gives way to irrational despondence, which in turn evolves into a new wave of irrational exuberance. In the old days (that is, the 20th century), these irrational uptrends and downtrends transitioned over months or years. In today's world, these booms and busts can occur on the same trading day. The almost-incomprehensible speed and volatility of market movements demonstrate convincingly that even the ivory tower experts of Wall Street have difficulty distinguishing fact from fiction and intellect from emotion. As Main Street investors trying to navigate the treacherous terrain of Wall Street, the best tactic we can employ to ensure our success is to stay informed and fully understand the risks and opportunities of investing.

In addition to the certainties of death and taxes, the only thing you can count on is that the future will be nothing like the past. Mutual fund companies and brokerage firms try to reinforce that idea (and do a little CYA damage control) by plastering this caveat on all their marketing materials: "Past performance is not indicative of future results." The flipside is that the more you understand past performance—and its accompanying facts and fictions—the more likely you are to achieve future results you can live with happily.

Balancing Risk and Reward

In his classic book on money management, *The Four Pillars of Investing,* William Bernstein describes two kinds of risk: "short term and long term. Short-term risk is the knot we get in our stomachs when our portfolios lose 20% or 40% in value over the course of a year or two. It is a fearsome thing." Bernstein goes on to explain, "Strangely, human beings are not as emotionally disturbed by long-term risk as they are by short term risk." Bernstein's observation is particularly relevant in today's times when the ravages of short-term risk are still fresh in everyone's mind. Unfortunately, this short-term focus has not raised awareness of the various other types of risk that every investor encounters.

Risk is an essential ingredient in investing. There is a direct correlation between risk and reward, and there is no such thing as a risk-free investment. There are investments that guarantee a return of principal and a certain rate of return over a specified period of time, but even those are not truly risk-free as they are encumbered by inflationary, liquidity, and interest-rate risks. The key is not to avoid risk, but rather to understand it and manage it at a level that is comfortable and appropriate.

Here are the major risk factors you need to understand and manage:

> ▷ **Market risk (also known as systemic risk):** This is the fundamental risk you take on whenever you purchase a stock, bond, or mutual fund. Most simply, it is the risk that your

investment will lose some or all of its value. A diversified portfolio provides the best protection against market risk.

▷ **Inflation risk:** This is the loss of purchasing power of your portfolio due to rising prices and is often associated with fixed-income investments. The longer the duration of a given fixed-income investment, the more inflation risk you're taking on. That's partly why a five-year CD pays more than a one-year CD. The latter has very little inflation risk, whereas the former is saddled with it. Hard assets like gold, commodities, and real estate are often used as a hedge against inflation.

▷ **Interest-rate risk:** This risk applies to fixed-income investments like bonds and is typically measured by the bond's duration (or maturity date). Because bonds and interest rates have an inverse relationship, bond prices will move down as interest rates rise. Short-term bonds with a maturity of one to three years suffer little from interest rate risk; longer-term bonds that stretch out 10, 20, or 30 years have significant interest rate risk.

▷ **Liquidity risk:** Although it's easy to buy most any kind of security, that's not always the case when you're trying to sell. Unlike stocks where there are live bid-ask prices pretty much every moment of the day, assets like corporate bonds and real estate exchange hands only rarely. Liquidity risk means you may have to sell your holding at a discount in order to attract buyers. Investing in mutual funds or ETFs can largely eliminate this risk from your portfolio.

▷ **Credit risk:** When you purchase a bond or bond mutual fund, you are essentially loaning money to the issuer. Credit risk is the risk that a bond issuer will not be able to pays its debts (either interest payments or redemption of principal at maturity). In the case of U.S. government bonds (such as Treasuries or Agencies), there is no credit risk. As a result, government bonds tend to pay lower interest rates than corporate bonds. The more credit risk you take on, the higher the interest rate you should receive.

▷ **Currency risk:** Currency risk refers to the fluctuation of exchange rates between different currencies like the U.S. dollar, the Japanese yen, and the British pound. As the global economy becomes increasingly intertwined, currency risk becomes a bigger and more important issue. Large multinational U.S.-based companies like Coca-Cola, IBM, and Johnson and Johnson receive substantial revenues from their overseas business, and the relative value of the dollar versus the local currency can boost or diminish their profitability. Similarly, international mutual funds can fluctuate just as much due to currency valuation as they do to fundamental changes in the underlying companies' business.

▷ **Longevity risk:** Traditionally, longevity risk was solely a concern of annuity companies and pension funds. The risk was that increased life expectancy of their policyholders and pensioners would result in payments that were substantially higher than what the actuaries had originally calculated. Today, longevity risk is increasingly used in relation to individuals and whether their savings are sufficient to sustain them through a longer-than-expected lifetime. As counterintuitive as it may sound, longevity risk should make you consider taking on a bit more of the previously mentioned investing risks. That's because the longer you live, the less likely it is that low-risk investments like CDs and Treasuries will be able to sustain an acceptable standard of living.

How and Why Averages Lie

If Mark Twain were alive today, he'd probably modify his well-known aphorism about the three most prevalent types of lies to read like this: "Lies, damn lies, and mutual fund performance." When times are good, mutual fund companies love to tout their performance numbers and Morningstar ratings. (When times are bad, on the other hand, they focus on their service levels or years of experience.) Performance is an unequivocally important aspect of mutual funds, and we would not suggest that you exclude it from your purchasing decision. We simply want to ensure that you understand the numbers, recognize when you're being misled (purposely or not), and consider performance as one consideration among many.

First, you need to understand the math behind performance numbers. Performance is almost always quoted as an "average" return—or a "mean," as you may recall from grade school. There are, however, two types of means: arithmetic and geometric. An arithmetic mean is calculated by adding all the values in a series and then dividing by the number of values in that series. It's how a baseball player's batting average is determined: the number of hits divided by the number of at-bats. When it comes to calculating investment performance, an arithmetic mean is pretty much meaningless.

Consider this example. You invest $100 in a mutual fund. At the end of the first year, the fund was up 100 percent and is now worth $200. In the second year the fund loses 50 percent of its value and is back down to $100. If you calculate the arithmetic mean, the average annual return would equal 25 percent. But that's clearly incorrect, because you haven't earned a penny. The problem is that investments grow in a multiplicative manner, not in an additive manner. When numbers are added together (as with batting averages), calculating the arithmetic mean is appropriate. When numbers are multiplied in sequence (as with the growth of an investment), the geometric mean (also called the Compound Annual Growth Rate) is the appropriate measure. We're highlighting the distinction between arithmetic and geometric means because the arithmetic means will *always* overstate the actual annualized return. Moreover, the overstatement increases as the variability of returns increases; in other words, arithmetic means are especially irrelevant for equity mutual funds, high-yield bond funds, REIT funds, and similar volatile asset classes. Calculating a geometric mean requires some heavy lifting and a financial calculator, but mutual fund companies are required to provide this measure as part of their "standardized performance," which is available in the fund's prospectus. So make sure you read the fine print.

The Whole Is Often Greater Than the Sum of Its Parts

Of course even when the math is accurately calculated as a geometric mean, the performance numbers reported by fund companies can still be misleading or open to misinterpretation. Consider this example of the ABC Growth Fund:

	Year 1	Year 2	Year 3	3-Year CAGR
ABC Growth Fund	+35%	-3%	-1%	9.04%

In its first year of existence, the ABC Growth Fund returned a whopping 35 percent. In the second year it lost 3 percent, and it lost another 1 percent in the third year. Over the three-year period, the fund returned a very respectable 9.04 percent average annualized return. The ABC Fund Company would not be shy—nor acting counter to its regulatory obligations—about promoting the 9.04-percent compound annual growth rate in promotional literature. The average investor who sees the three-year number would likely be impressed and want to get in on the action. After all, who wouldn't want an investment that earns more than 9 percent per year? With just a little more dig-ging, however, the investor would see that anyone who bought the fund after the first year didn't come close to realizing a 9-percent gain and, to the contrary, actually lost money. And the saddest part of this is that, invariably, the majority of ABC Growth Fund shareholders bought the fund in years two and three, having been seduced by the lure of robust performance. The only consolation we can offer these late-to-the-party shareholders is that they are not alone.

Why Your Performance Lags Your Mutual Fund

Over the years, there's been a lot of anecdotal conjecture that indi-vidual investors tend to chase performance and, as a result, buy high and sell low. The first solid evidence of this tendency came to light after the tech bubble of 2000–2001. Jason Zweig, a financial writer formerly with *Money* magazine and now with *The Wall Street Journal,* wrote an eye-opening article in 2002 comparing the stated returns of numerous mutual funds versus what the typical shareholder experienced. Zweig looked at the period from 1998 through 2001 and found that "while the average fund generated a 5.7% annualized total return over the four years, the average fund investor earned just 1%." The reality was even worse for investors in high-growth mutual funds. In examining the per-formance of the Janus Funds family, Zweig estimates that the "average portfolio returned 5% annually from 1998 through 2001, but the typi-cal fund investor at Janus lost an annual average of 11.1%."

The fund companies don't cause this imbalance, and they are not improperly communicating their performance record. The problem lies with investors themselves. Few investors do sufficient homework before investing in a particular fund or security. They rarely read the prospectus or annual report. Except for the small minority of people who have a written investment strategy, most investment decisions are made quickly and impulsively based on little more than a "hot tip" or a favorable mention in a publication or news program. The same people who spend hours researching the difference between plasma, LCD, and DLP wide-screen televisions or comparing the features, energy usage, and reliability of a $500 washing machine will make a $10,000 investment in a mutual fund with nary a thought.

So, instead of doing their homework, most investors look at past performance, are enticed by big numbers, and jump in—usually at the worst possible time. The problem has gotten so severe that Morningstar now calculates and publicizes "investor returns" alongside a fund's standardized performance numbers. Morningstar offers this service because, in the firm's own words, "Investors often suffer from poor timing and poor planning. Investors know they should hold diversified portfolios, but many chase past performance and end up buying funds too late or selling too soon." Investor returns take into account cash flows into and out of funds, calculate "dollar-weighted" and "time-weighted" returns, and better reflect the performance that the average investor achieved.

Whether you consult Morningstar's investor returns, review a fund's year-by-year track record, or read the prospectus, take a breath before you invest. If the mutual fund is a good buy today, it will still be a good buy tomorrow. Take a moment to write down three reasons why the fund (or individual security) fits into your overall strategy. And before you buy, have an exit strategy. Will you sell the fund if it drops 10 percent or 20 percent? Will you sell half your position if the fund increases by 40 percent? Interestingly, in addition to chasing hot performers, investors are loath to sell their dogs. Psychologically, they desperately want to hold on until the fund gets back to even. They fail to investigate whether there are specific reasons for the fund's underperformance (for example, a change in portfolio managers or a change in strategy or methodology). In addition, by sticking with a losing investment, they miss out on the opportunity to put their money to work elsewhere. This concept of lost opportunities is not a rationale or recommendation for market-timing. Rather, it's an acknowledgment that the markets move in waves, and those waves often last years or decades. Instead of allowing the waves to continually knock you over, position yourself to catch the curl and enjoy the ride.

Recovering From Market Setbacks

When asked what the stock market will do, John Pierpont Morgan, one of America's great financiers, replied, "It will fluctuate." With fluctuation comes inevitable losses, and, although the stock market devastation of 2008 made people acutely aware of the magnitude of losses they could suffer, most investors don't fully understand the math of recovery. Because of the geometric relationship between losses and subsequent gains, the percentage gain required to offset a loss is significantly higher than the original loss. The following table shows that even a moderate loss of 20 percent requires a 25-percent gain to recover to a breakeven balance. And with recent losses at the 30-percent to 50-percent levels, investors would have to experience outsized gains to get back to even.

Loss	10%	20%	30%	40%	50%
Needed Gain to Break Even	11%	25%	43%	67%	100%

The next table looks at this issue from a slightly different perspective. In this example, you've experienced a three-year string of strong performance and are averaging a 15-percent return. In the fourth year, the market drops 15 percent. In order to get back to the previous high point, experienced at the end of the third year, you'd need an 18-percent return. However, in order to get the portfolio back to a 15-percent average return, you would need a 56-percent gain in the fifth year.

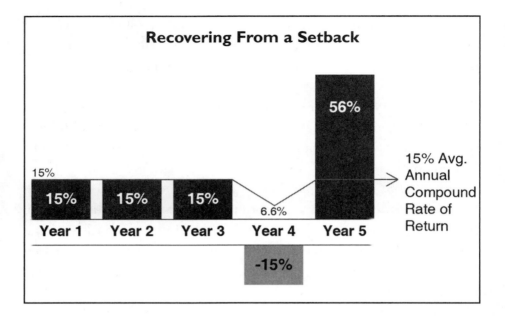

The preceding graphic is a generic illustration designed to make the concept easy to visualize and understand. In order to make the concept even more meaningful, however, the next graphic looks at actual returns from 2005 through 2008. (Warning: This is not for the faint of heart.)

The years 2005 to 2007 each delivered positive returns for the S&P 500. At the end of that three-year period, stocks (and their shareholders) enjoyed an 8.62-percent average annualized return. The economic world changed frighteningly in 2008, and the S&P 500 dropped 37 percent. In order to fully recover from 2008's losses and bring the five-year annualized return back to 8.62 percent, the S&P 500 would have to increase by 87.5 percent in 2009. Anyone willing to wager on the likelihood of that occurrence has more in common with Las Vegas than Wall Street.

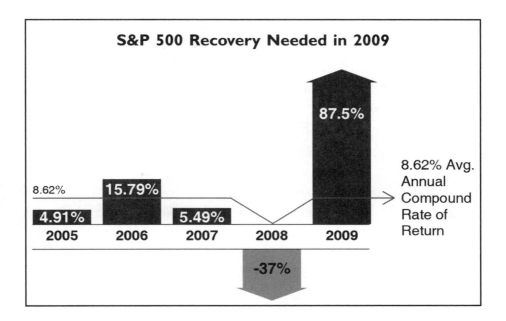

The good news is that these gains do not have to occur overnight. The critical thing is to not obsess over your losses and waver from your long-term strategy in order to hit it big. If your losses were due to taking on too much risk, adjust your portfolio to match your temperament and time frame. In some cases you simply will not be able to fully recover without exposing yourself to additional, unwanted risk. As difficult as it may be, you need to accept the loss and focus on avoiding additional losses, managing risk, and generating steady growth in the future.

Recovering From Market Setbacks in Retirement

The primary goal of a retirement portfolio is very simple: avoid losing money. In years like 2008, however, when there was no place to hide, losses are unavoidable. And although losses are troublesome at any point in one's investing career, they are especially problematic during the income-generation phase of retirement. A retirement portfolio—which is producing income via annual withdrawals—faces a much steeper climb to get back to even after a loss than does a buy-and-hold portfolio. For example, in order to recover from a 20-percent loss, a buy-and-hold portfolio needs to average a 4.6-percent annual return over five years. A retirement portfolio in withdrawal mode, however, must generate a 12.5-percent average annual return over five years to restore the account to its pre-loss balance. (You can, of course, make the argument that there is no need for a retirement portfolio to "get back to even," as the portfolio value will naturally decline from year to year. Although that is technically true, we believe income investors need to understand the seriously negative impact of market downturns—if only to take additional precautions to protect their portfolio from major setbacks.)

The tables that follow on page 157 provide a detailed comparison of the returns necessary to restore a portfolio to its original value after a decline. Notice that a withdrawal portfolio can be viewed as being in "recovery mode" even if it's recovering from a positive return (that is, 5 percent or 2 percent). This is because the annual return has to exceed the withdrawal rate (which increases each year for inflation) in order to maintain a constant balance.

The obvious point is that it's difficult to recover from moderate losses and virtually impossible to recover from large ones. The trick is to build a portfolio that can avoid significant losses and, if losses happen nonetheless, has a reasonable chance of getting you back to even. Toward that end, we compared four sample portfolios: 100-percent large-cap U.S. equity, 100-percent U.S. intermediate bond, a traditional 60-percent equity/40-percent bond mix, and a global multi-asset portfolio. (See the table on page 158). The first two portfolios—100-percent stocks and 100-percent bonds—are very unlikely strategies for retirement, but we include them to further our book-long mantra about the benefits of diversification.

Needed Average Annual % Return to Restore Original Portfolio Balance

Portfolio return from which a recovery is needed	Withdrawal Retirement Portfolio $500,000 initial balance, first-year withdrawal of 5% of initial balance, 3% increase of annual withdrawal				
	Within 1 Year	Within 2 Years	Within 3 Years	Within 4 Years	Within 5 Years
5%	5.2%	5.2%	5.3%	5.4%	5.5%
2%	8.4%	6.9%	6.4%	6.3%	6.2%
0%	10.7%	8.0%	7.2%	6.9%	6.7%
-2%	13.1%	9.2%	8.0%	7.5%	7.2%
-5%	16.8%	11.1%	9.3%	8.4%	8.0%
-10%	23.7%	14.4%	11.5%	10.1%	9.4%
-15%	31.4%	18.0%	13.9%	12.0%	10.9%
-20%	40.2%	22.0%	16.5%	14.0%	12.5%
-25%	50.2%	26.4%	19.4%	16.1%	14.3%
-30%	61.8%	31.3%	22.6%	18.5%	16.2%
-35%	75.3%	36.9%	26.1%	21.2%	18.4%

Portfolio return from which a recovery is needed	Buy-and-Hold Portfolio				
	Within 1 Year	Within 2 Years	Within 3 Years	Within 4 Years	Within 5 Years
-2%	2.0%	1.0%	0.7%	0.5%	0.4%
-5%	5.3%	2.6%	1.7%	1.3%	1.0%
-10%	11.1%	5.4%	3.6%	2.7%	2.1%
-15%	17.6%	8.5%	5.6%	4.1%	3.3%
-20%	25.0%	11.8%	7.7%	5.7%	4.6%
-25%	33.3%	15.5%	10.1%	7.5%	5.9%
-30%	42.9%	19.5%	12.6%	9.3%	7.4%
-35%	53.8%	24.0%	15.4%	11.4%	9.0%

The average annualized return of the all-stock portfolio from 1970 to 2008 was 9.48 percent. During that 39-year period, a buy-and-hold portfolio composed of 100-percent U.S. large-cap stocks offered an 80-percent chance of recovering from a 10-percent portfolio loss within five years. That same portfolio in a withdrawal mode had only a 63-percent probability of recovery.

Model Portfolios (1970–2008)	39-Year Annualized Return (%)	Probability of recovery from a 10% loss within 5 years in a Buy-and-Hold Portfolio	Probability of recovery from a 10% loss within 5 years in a Withdrawal Portfolio (5% initial withdrawal rate, 3% COLA)
100% Large U.S. Stock *(S&P 500 Index)*	9.48	80	63
100% U.S. Bonds *(Intermediate Bond Index)*	8.13	100	29
Traditional 60% Equity/40% Bond *(600% S&P 500, 40% U.S. Bonds)*	9.35	94	63
Global Multi-Asset *(14.3% in each of the following: Large U.S. Stock, Small U.S. Stock, Non-U.S. Stock, U.S. Bonds, Cash, REITs, Commodities)*	10.21	97	74

For a portfolio consisting entirely of intermediate term U.S. bonds, the chance of recovery from a 10-percent loss was 100 percent within five years in a buy-and-hold portfolio but only 29 percent in a withdrawal portfolio. An offsetting virtue of an all-bond portfolio is that the one-year returns are almost always positive. So although an all-bond withdrawal portfolio doesn't recover well from losses, it very rarely experiences losses. Indeed, during this 39-year period, the only negative return for an all-bond portfolio was -1.8 percent in 1994.

The next portfolio represents a traditional balanced portfolio with an asset mix of 60-percent equity and 40-percent bonds. It delivered a 9.35-percent annualized return over the 39-year period (assuming annual rebalancing to keep the portfolio proportions constant over time). In a buy-and-hold situation, the traditional balanced portfolio had a 94-percent chance of recovery from a 10-percent loss within five years and a 63-percent chance of recovery in a withdrawal portfolio.

The fourth portfolio represents the true diversification of a global multi-asset strategy with equal 14.3-percent weighting of seven different classes: large-cap U.S. stocks, small-cap U.S. stocks, non-U.S. stocks, U.S. bonds, REITs, commodities, and cash. This portfolio was also assumed to be rebalanced annually so as to maintain the desired portfolio weightings. The 39-year average annualized return of the global multi-asset portfolio was 10.21 percent, meaningfully higher than any of the other portfolios. The probability of recovery from a 10-percent loss within five years in a buy-and-hold portfolio was 97 percent, just a shade behind the all-bond portfolio. In a withdrawal portfolio, the global multi-asset portfolio offered a 74-percent chance of recovery from a 10-percent loss within five years—dramatically higher than the all-bond portfolio and an appreciable improvement from the all-stock portfolio and the traditional balanced portfolio.

This analysis uses 5 percent as the initial withdrawal rate with a 3-percent rate of inflation for subsequent withdrawals. Different withdrawal rates and inflation assumptions would significantly change the results. If, for example, the initial withdrawal rate were 3 percent using the global multi-asset portfolio, the probability of recovery would increase from 74 percent to 91 percent. Alternatively, if the withdrawal rate were 8 percent, the chance of recovery would drop to 37 percent.

Reverse Dollar-Cost Averaging

Dollar-cost averaging is the sliced-bread marvel of investing. It helps you buy more shares when prices are low, reduces your cost basis, and provides a powerful springboard to double-digit returns when the market moves up. It's an essential element of investing in a 401(k) or IRA, and there is no downside to dollar-cost averaging when you're building wealth and saving for the future.

Unfortunately, it's a whole different ballgame when it comes to generating retirement income. Rather than being your ally, reverse dollar-cost averaging (so-called because you are regularly taking money out of the market rather than putting it in) is the enemy. Think about it like this: When you buy a stock or mutual fund at a depressed price, you're content to sit back and wait for the price to recover and generate a nice profit. However, when you sell a stock or fund at a low price, you're permanently locked out of receiving any future gain from those shares because you no longer own them.

Consider the accompanying table shown on page 161. In this example, you buy 50,000 shares of a mutual fund at $10.00, for a total investment of $500,000. You begin periodic withdrawals of $2,000. After your initial withdrawal of 200 shares at $10.00 each, the market begins a prolonged bear market and share prices slump as low at $7.00. As a result, subsequent withdrawals of $2,000 require more shares to be sold, reaching a high point of 286 shares when prices hit their low of $7.00. At the end of the 12-cycle withdrawal period, you've received $24,000 in benefits, but, instead of your account value equaling your contributions minus withdrawals ($476,000), it's only worth $422,739. And instead of

Reverse Dollar-Cost Averaging				
Account Value	Share Price	Investment/ Cost Basis	Shares Sold	Remaining Shares
$500,000		$500,000		50,000
$498,000	$10.00	−$2,000	−200	49,800
$421,300	$8.50	−$2,000	−235	49,565
$394,518	$8.00	−$2,000	−250	49,315
$367,860	$7.50	−$2,000	−267	49,048
$341,336	$7.00	−$2,000	−286	48,762
$339,336	$7.00	−$2,000	−286	48,477
$361,575	$7.50	−$2,000	−267	48,210
$383,680	$8.00	−$2,000	−250	47,960
$357,700	$7.50	−$2,000	−267	47,693
$379,546	$8.00	−$2,000	−250	47,443
$377,546	$8.00	−$2,000	−250	47,193
$422,739	$9.00	−$2,000	−222	46,971
$422,739		$476,000	−3,029	46,971

having sold 2,400 shares, the low prices have forced you to sell 3,029 shares. At this point, even if the share price returned to $10.00, your account would be worth only $469,710 for a net loss of $6,290. In other words, the $10.00 per share value of the 629 extra shares you were forced to sell is lost forever, and you have 629 fewer chances to make up for your losses.

Monte Carlo Simulations: Sure Thing or Sucker's Bet?

As we stated earlier, averages lie. Investments with similar "average returns" can deliver markedly different real returns due to the effects of compounding, volatility, and the sequence of returns. All those variables make average investment returns meaningless if not truly dangerous. Consider this non-financial example. The average annual wind speed in Tampa is 8.3 mph. However, if an architect were designing a new skyscraper for Tampa, he would face criminal charges if his building specifications were based on the average wind speed. Instead, architects in Tampa, Miami, and other coastal cities focus on constructing a building able to withstand hurricane-driven wind velocities. Investment planning, and retirement planning in particular, must be done with the same type of foresight and "worst-case" mindset.

That's why, over the last few years, Monte Carlo simulations have become a common tool among financial advisors. Monte Carlo simulations are named after the glamorous French Riviera city best known for gambling and over-the-top wealth. Like its namesake, the Monte Carlo method revolves around probability. Specifically, Monte Carlo methodologies were developed by mathematicians to approximate the probability of a desired outcome by running thousands of trial-run calculations using randomly generated variables. Financial advisors use Monte Carlo simulations to determine the probability of a particular investment plan succeeding for a given number of years. For example, a Monte Carlo simulation might demonstrate that a given retirement income plan has an 80-percent chance of succeeding through age 90.

As financial planning tools go, Monte Carlo simulations are a valuable step forward, but they must be accompanied by a number of caveats. Most importantly, the results suggest probability, not certainty, and most people are poorly equipped to understand the full meaning of the stated probability. Although an 80-percent chance of success would represent fabulous odds at the racetrack or casino, it doesn't sound all that appealing when applied to one's lifestyle. And even if 80 percent does represent an acceptable probability for satisfying your retirement dreams, would you be equally comfortable with a 20-percent failure rate? Furthermore, the 80-percent chance of success you were comfortable with at age 65 may prove terrifying a few years down the road.

Like many sophisticated tools or methodologies that get adapted for use by a different industry or mindset, Monte Carlo simulations are subject to error, misinterpretation, or misrepresentation. As co-author Craig Israelsen points out in a paper written for the Academy of Financial Services entitled "The Problem with Monte Carlo Simulations" (J. H. Bell and C. L. Israelsen):

> The detailed methodologies of most Monte Carlo approaches are developed by mathematicians intimately familiar with the science involved, but unfamiliar with the idiosyncrasies of financial analysis inputs. Conversely, these methodologies are used by financial analysts who are expert in these idiosyncrasies but unfamiliar with the mathematical principles involved. Neither can fully appreciate the problems of the other.

The positive aspects of Monte Carlo simulations are that they bring variability to the forefront of any discussion. There can be no certainty when investing. So, rather than suggesting you ignore the results of Monte Carlo simulations, we ask simply that you use the information as one input among many.

Chapter 11

I NSULATED:
Staying Cool During Volatile Markets

Lehman Brothers. Merrill Lynch. AIG. Morgan Stanley. Goldman Sachs. These giants of the American financial services industry collapsed or were brought to the brink of failure by ignoring the key tenet they preached to their clients: diversification. They made huge bets in a single asset class and, in so doing, created the breeding ground for a perfect storm of historic proportions.

In reality, of course, no investment portfolio can be viewed as truly "immune" from market volatility. Nor can any mix of asset classes be considered "infallible" in achieving one's financial goals and objectives. The best you can strive for is an investment mix that is "insulated" from radical swings in valuation and serves to smooth out the inevitable ups and downs of the financial markets. The most effective way to achieve the appropriate level of insulation is through maximum diversification within your investment portfolio.

Diversification has often been called the free lunch of investing, and experts agree that it is the single best way to even out the roller-coaster ride of the markets. They differ, however, on the definition of diversification and how best to achieve it. The ironic thing is that most people—including the savviest individual investors and most learned financial services professionals—believe they're diversified even when they're not. One of the nation's largest and most respected mutual fund companies, Franklin-Templeton, recently ran a series of ads touting the benefits of diversification. To illustrate their point, the ad included a photograph of three Dalmatians sitting side by side. One was totally black, one was white with black spots, and one was all white. At first glance, the trio might appear to represent diversification—but the Franklin-Templeton marketers seemed to ignore the fact that all three animals were Dalmatians. A better illustration would have been a dachshund, a Dalmatian, and a St. Bernard. That would have been better, but still not particularly diverse as all three images remained dogs.

The next logical step up the diversification ladder might be an illustration of a turtle, a Dalmatian, and an elephant. Better—but they're still all animals. So what should Franklin-Templeton have illustrated? We would suggest something along the lines of a Dalmatian alongside a pumpkin and a rock. Such a threesome would represent the virtues of *true* diversification rather than the overly simplistic mix of stocks and bonds and cash that passes for diversification in most financial portfolios. (It's also interesting how well this analogy aligns with the "animal, vegetable, mineral" approach to problem-solving that typifies parlor games like "20 Questions." Perhaps it is true that everything we need to know we learned in kindergarten.)

Modern Portfolio Theory and the Efficient Frontier

Modern Portfolio Theory, or MPT, as it is commonly known, is the grand-daddy of asset allocation and diversification strategies. MPT was introduced in 1952 by a young University of Chicago doctoral candidate, Harry Markowitz. Thirty-eight years later Dr. Markowitz received a Nobel Prize for his seminal work in helping investors insulate themselves from market turbulence.

MPT espouses two central tenets. The first tenet is that it is difficult, if not impossible, to beat the market. By this, Dr. Markowitz was suggesting that most stock pickers will not be able to consistently beat a broad sample of stocks (or, in today's terms, a stock market "index"). The second tenet states that it is nevertheless possible to construct an optimal portfolio—in other words, a portfolio that will provide the maximum return for a given level of risk. Let's take a closer look at each of these tenets.

Beating the market consistently is next to impossible because of the wide variety of risks associated with investing. Markowitz identified and grouped these assorted risks into two categories:

- ▷ **Systematic Risks:** These are macro-economic risk factors that cannot be diversified away. Examples include interest rates, inflation, recessions, natural disasters, wars, and other geo-political considerations. Systematic risk provides the underpinnings for the "rising tide lifts all boats" aphorism and its bearish counterpart.

- ▷ **Unsystematic Risks:** These are the specific risks associated with owning specific securities. Examples include poor management (General Motors), lagging technology (Polaroid), fraud (Enron), and operational inefficiencies (U.S. airlines other than Southwest and JetBlue). Unsystematic risk can be diversified away simply by increasing the number of stocks in your portfolio and serves as the basis for the "don't put all your eggs in one basket" aphorism.

According to Markowitz and MPT, systematic risk is ever-present and cannot be avoided. If you can't deal with the inherent risks of the market, then stash all your cash in CDs and T-bills. You'll still face the inflationary risk of reduced buying power, but your portfolio will never "appear" to decrease in value. For the vast majority of investors, systematic risk is something to recognize but not obsess over.

Unsystematic risk, however, deserves your undivided attention. This is where fortunes are made and lost. And, in keeping with the I-centric parlance of this book, this is where you can idiot-proof your portfolio. You do so with another critical I-factor: indexing. Rather than struggling to determine whether Merck will outperform Pfizer or whether Target will gain market share from Walmart, you simply buy all four, along with the rest of the market, in the form of index funds or ETFs.

The big question, of course, is this: How does "buying the market" protect you from the gyrations of the market? Inasmuch as there are many markets, the key to insulating your portfolio is to invest in more than one "market." A portfolio that invests in multiple markets (or more accurately a portfolio that invests in multiple asset classes) is far more insulated from losses because not all asset classes move up and down at the same time.

Think of it as the way a vaccine protects you from a given disease. Typically the vaccine includes a tiny dose of the very disease that you're trying to prevent. However, by exposing the body to the "disease risk" in a diluted form, you strengthen your defenses should you be exposed to a full-dose attack. Similarly, by exposing yourself to the risk of buying both Merck and Pfizer, you avoid the risk of buying just one of them, and you strengthen your defenses should one of them fail miserably.

Having won the Nobel Prize for his work, it should come as no surprise that Markowitz explains his theory quite eloquently via the "Efficient Frontier"—which you can consider as the game plan for converting MPT from theory to action. Let's start with two securities—Security 1 and Security 2—and plot them on a graph where the vertical axis equals return and the horizontal axis equals risk (as measured by "standard deviation of return"). If you only consider the rate of return, then a portfolio split 50-50 between the two securities would return precisely the average of the two.

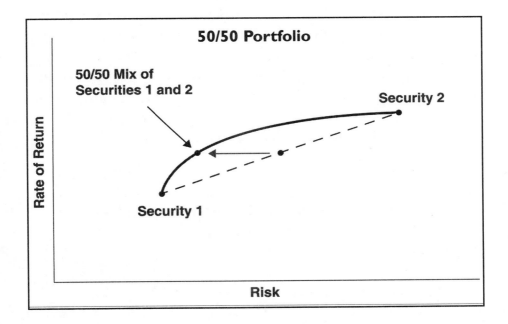

An interesting thing happens, however, when you add risk (or standard deviation) to the mix. Whereas the annual rate-of-return will typically equal the average of the two securities, the standard deviation of the 50-50 portfolio will almost always be lower than the average risk level of the two securities. That translates into good news for the investor by providing the same return for less risk. As an investor, you always want to be as high up and as far left as possible in the risk-return continuum—in other words, reaping as much gain from as little risk as possible.

As part of his research, Markowitz tested the Efficient Frontier using 11 different portfolio combinations of stocks and bonds. Starting with a portfolio of 100-percent bonds (at the bottom left of the chart), he added stocks to and removed bonds from the portfolio in 10-percent allotments, ending with a portfolio of 100-percent stocks (at the upper right). The resulting Efficient Frontier, using several decades' worth of performance data, is an upward sloping curve that clearly demonstrates the increased reward that comes with increased risk. What it also shows, however, is that the risk-reward tradeoff reaches a point of diminishing returns. Whereas adding stocks to the all-bond portfolio has an immediate and dramatic effect on returns while taking on a minimal amount of additional risk, the benefits of moving from 70-percent stocks to 100-percent stocks are marginal on the performance side of the equation while significantly increasing the risk of the portfolio.

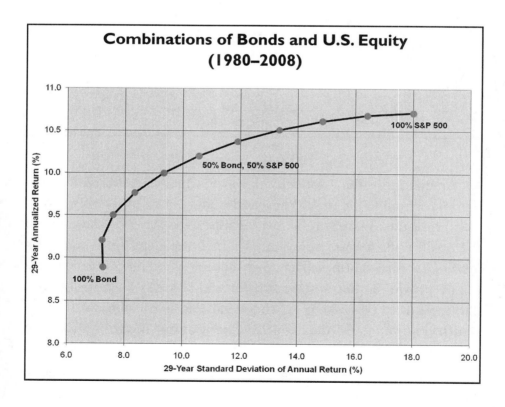

Risk: A Counterintuitive Perspective

The key reason most investors are not sufficiently diversified is that they fear risk. Once they venture outside the "norm" of U.S. stocks, U.S. bonds, and cash, they begin to worry about taking on too much risk. More adventurous investors might take a small position in international stocks, but that's about as far as it usually goes. And that's unfortunate because, as counterintuitive as it sounds, adding riskier asset classes to an investment portfolio can actually serve to reduce the risk of the entire portfolio. As with most things in life, adding a little spice to your investment portfolio makes it a lot easier to live with and enjoy.

Effective portfolio construction is not unlike the recipe for a world-class salsa. The main ingredient in salsa is, of course, tomatoes. As important as they are, it's the "hot and spicy" ingredients that separate good salsa from great salsa. Even though we many never want to eat the hot and spicy ingredients individually, we don't hesitate to add them to salsa. This metaphor works perfectly when building investment portfolios. Some assets might appear too risky (or volatile) to invest in individually, but when combined with other assets they actually lower the risk of the overall portfolio.

Consider the example shown on page 171. For many investors, the years 2000, 2001, and 2002 were a nightmare. Why? Because they got caught in a trap. The trap was believing that one particular asset class will always outperform the others. As shown in the accompanying table, from 1995 to 1999 the U.S. stock market (as measured by the S&P 500 Index) was cranking out annual returns of more than 20 percent each year. A lot of investors loaded up on U.S. stock just in time for three consecutive negative years. A more balanced portfolio would have included bonds, cash, real estate, and commodities (the spicy stuff).

Notice how bonds did well in 2000, 2001, and 2002. So did real estate. Commodities performed extremely well in 2000 and 2002, but tripped in 2001. The key point is that diversification would have avoided or minimized the nasty losses experienced by stock (U.S. stock and non-U.S. stock) in 2000–2002.

Annual Returns of Various Investment Assets

Year	Large U.S. Equity	Small U.S. Equity	Non-U.S. Equity	Intermediate Term U.S. Bonds	Cash	Real Estate	Commodities	Equally Weighted Multi-Asset Portfolio
1995	37.58	28.45	11.21	14.41	5.79	12.24	20.33	18.57
1996	22.96	16.49	6.05	4.06	5.26	37.05	33.92	17.97
1997	33.36	22.36	1.78	7.72	5.31	19.66	-14.07	10.87
1998	28.58	-2.55	20	8.49	5.02	-17	-35.75	0.97
1999	21.04	21.26	26.97	0.49	4.87	-2.58	40.92	16.14
2000	-9.1	-3.02	-14.17	10.47	6.32	31.04	49.74	10.18
2001	-11.89	2.49	-21.44	8.42	3.67	12.35	-31.93	-5.48
2002	-22.1	-20.48	-15.94	9.64	1.68	3.58	32.07	-1.65
2003	28.69	47.25	38.59	2.29	1.05	36.18	20.72	24.97
2004	10.88	18.33	20.25	2.33	1.43	33.16	17.28	14.81
2005	4.91	4.55	13.54	1.68	3.34	13.82	25.55	9.63
2006	15.79	18.37	26.34	3.84	5.07	35.97	-15.09	12.9
2007	5.49	-1.57	11.17	8.47	4.77	-17.6	32.67	6.21
2008	-37	-33.79	-43.38	10.43	1.51	-39.2	-46.49	-26.85

The far-right column of the accompanying table shows the annual performance of a diversified portfolio with equal portions of six assets. In 2000, U.S. and non-U.S. stocks got hammered, but the diversified portfolio (with its spicy ingredients) had a return of more than 10 percent. In 2001, even a diversified portfolio got stung with a loss of nearly 6 percent. That's reality. Diversification does not eliminate losses, but it does minimize them. In 2002, broad diversification insulated the portfolio from a serious loss. An overall portfolio return in 2002 of -1.65 percent is far better than the losses experienced in the individual "stock" assets. Large U.S. stocks lost 22.1 percent, small U.S. stocks lost 20.48 percent, and non-U.S. stocks lost 15.94%.

The year 2008 was a different experience (and one that you will probably never forget!). Broad diversification helped but didn't sidestep the carnage. An equally weighted seven-asset portfolio lost 26.85 percent, but that was "better" than the heavy losses sustained by large, small, and non-U.S. stocks. The real difference in 2008 was the inability of real estate and commodities to zig when stocks zagged. That doesn't happen very often, and that's precisely why this multi-asset portfolio took a hit in 2008.

More Can Equal Less

The most common way investors try to diversify their portfolios is by investing in a lot of mutual funds. It seems logical that owning more funds would spread your money out over a larger number of securities and thereby increase diversity and decrease volatility. As logical as it sounds, in most cases this approach has the opposite result. Why? Because people tend to "diversify" among different funds but neglect to diversify among different asset classes. Owning three different large-cap growth funds accomplishes next to nothing. They all have the same mandate, and their portfolio managers are all trying to outfox the other— and they all end up having a mix of stocks that look eerily similar. Take a look at the semi-annual reports or prospectuses of any three large-cap growth funds and you'll be astounded by the amount of overlap. In many cases, the top 10 holdings of each fund will be identical. That shouldn't be a surprise. With the increased transparency of corporate revenue and income streams, the best-in-class high-growth companies will be well known to every portfolio manager—and every manager will want to own them in his or her portfolio or risk putting up performance numbers lower than the rival manager and thus lowering his/her performance bonus.

If you're making the mistake of investing in commissionable mutual funds, your mistake is worsened by buying multiple funds within the same asset class. That's because you may be losing out on the "breakpoints" many fund companies offer their larger shareholders. Let's assume you have $100,000 to invest in a large-cap growth fund. You're working with a commissioned broker, buying "A-shares," and the front-end load begins at 5 percent but drops to 4 percent for investments over $25,000. If you purchased four different funds from four different fund families, you would be charged commissions of $5,000. If, however, you invested all $100,000 in a single fund, your total commission would be reduced to $4,250.

The reason investors buy too many funds is concern about choosing the "wrong" fund. They figure they can improve their chances of getting a big winner by spreading their money around. That thought process is fundamentally flawed because it's focused on "beating the market." True diversification is focused not on beating the market but rather on ensuring exposure to whatever asset class is "beating the market" at any given point in time. The winning approach to investing is not to own three or four large-cap growth funds, but to own one large-cap growth fund, one large-cap value fund, one small-cap fund, and so on. And if you can't decide which fund to select, then go with inexpensive index funds or exchange traded funds (or ETFs).

Consider this lumber metaphor to help create a visual of the power of diversification. A glue-laminated wood beam is much stronger than a solid wood beam of the same size precisely because the laminated beam comprises layers of wood with differing grain patterns. It is the diversity of the components that gives the 'glulam' its strength. In like manner, the strength and durability of a retirement portfolio comes from adding diverse components.

Correlation: The Secret Ingredient of Diversification

Correlation is the word used to describe how one investment goes up and down compared to another investment. The mathematical range of correlation is from +1.00 to -1.00. If the prices of two investments move together almost identically over the same time period, then the correlation between them will be close to a 100-percent positive correlation, or +1.00. Conversely, if two investments tend to move in opposite directions, they are said to be "inversely correlated," and their correlation would approach -1.00. A correlation of zero indicates that the relative behavior between the two investments is essentially random with no discernable pattern.

Before discussing how correlation works in the investment world, consider this simple analogy illustrating the importance of low correlation among the components of a system. For example, a basketball team needs players with different attributes and talents; they need a diversified team. Building a basketball team with five point guards would not be a great idea, as much as we value point guards. A center is needed, as well as several forwards. Because they have different attributes and talents, the correlation between point guards and power forwards is quite low—and low correlation is what we're after. So whereas two twin brothers, who both play point guard, would have a correlation close to +1.00, a left-handed 6-foot-1-inch tall point guard and a right-handed 7-foot-4-inch center would have a correlation approaching -1.00. By combining the two, you have a better chance at beating the opposition regardless of what they throw at you offensively or defensively.

The next two graphics illustrate how correlation affects the performance of an investment portfolio. In the first illustration, Investment A and Investment B both move up and down in virtually identical fashion, but Investment B has a lower return than Investment A. When the two investments are combined, the risk behavior is the same, and the returns of the resulting portfolio equal the average of the two, with identical up and down trends. As a result, combining Investment A with Investment B provides no diversification benefits, and portfolio risk and volatility are unchanged.

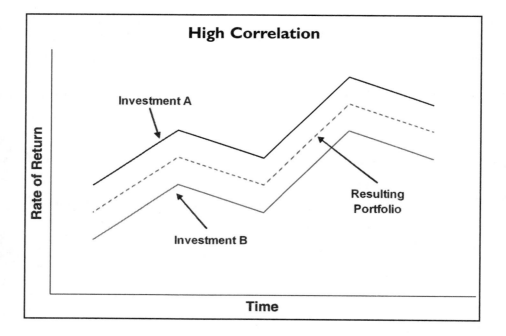

In the second illustration, however, Investment E and Investment F move in opposite directions and have a correlation close to -1.00. An easy way to think about this is to imagine that Investment E is an airline stock, and Investment F is an oil company stock. When oil prices are high, the oil companies reap huge profits, driving up the price of their stock. At the same time, high oil prices lead to higher costs for airplane fuel. This tends to make the airline stocks go down because they have to raise ticket prices, thereby selling fewer tickets and lessening their profits. By combining these two investments in a portfolio, the vast majority of volatility is eradicated and you enjoy steady and stable growth. Keep in mind, however, that we're illustrating an optimal hypothetical situation. In real life, absolute negative correlation is very rare.

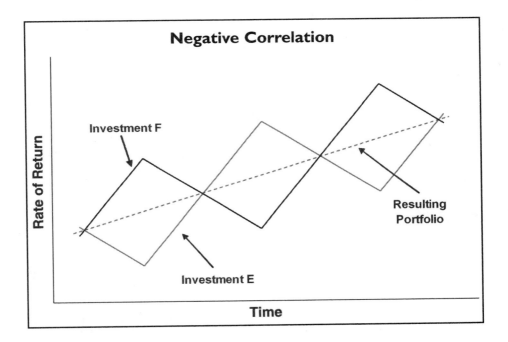

Although absolute negative correlation is a rarity, it is actually quite easy to add low-correlating and negative-correlating assets to your portfolio and achieve a significant diversification benefit. The chart that follows shows the correlation factors between various asset classes. What you see in the far-left column of the chart is a high correlation of small-cap U.S. stocks (0.78) and developed country international stocks (0.66) to U.S. large-cap stocks. This means that adding those asset classes alone does little to properly diversify your portfolio. Unfortunately, those are the asset classes (along with U.S. bonds, which do have a negative correlation to large-caps) used by most investors to broaden their diversification. True diversification can be achieved by adding asset classes that have low correlation to large U.S. stock, such as commodities (-0.07), real estate (0.50), bonds (0.16), and cash (0.15). Blending all seven assets together creates a portfolio with an average correlation of 0.19—which is a wonderfully low correlation.

39-Year Correlation of Annual Returns
(1970–2008)

	Large U.S. Equity	Small U.S. Equity	Non-U.S. Equity	U.S. Bonds	Cash	REIT
Small U.S. Equity	0.78					
Non-U.S. Equity	0.66	0.54				
U.S /bonds	0.16	0.02	-0.12			
Cash	0.15	0.09	-0.01	0.39		
REIT	0.50	0.75	0.37	0.15	0.15	
Commodities	-0.07	-0.15	0.03	-0.09	-0.09	-0.04

The power of a diversified investment strategy using correlation as a primary factor is demonstrated in the following graph. Over the 10-year period from 1999 through the end of 2008, a portfolio composed of the seven asset classes listed in the prior correlation table, dramatically outperformed an Efficient Frontier composed of stocks and bonds while also moderating the overall risk level. More return than an all-stock portfolio with less risk than an all-stock portfolio: the ultimate goal of virtually every investor.

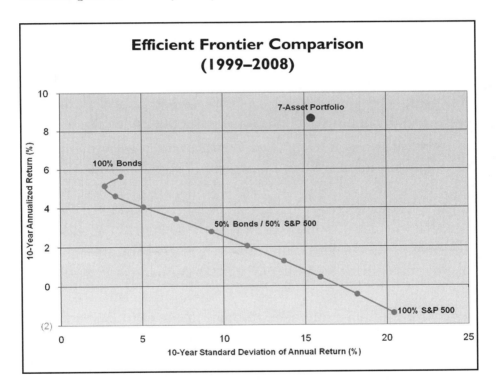

Portfolio Insulation and Your Retirement Income Stream

As important as diversification and non-correlation are to the asset accumulation stage of life, it strikes us as odd that the financial press has not paid more attention to their benefits during the income-generation phase. We suggest that diversification is an important risk management tool during retirement because retirees have less time to make up for market losses. And it's precisely that lack of time that makes "risk-of-loss" a vitally important consideration.

The table that follows displays the performance results of three different portfolios during the "distribution" period when money is being systematically withdrawn (such as during retirement).

This analysis contrasts the performance of the equally weighted multi-asset portfolio against a 60/40 portfolio and a 40/60 portfolio. The 60/40 portfolio represents a 60-percent equity and 40-percent fixed income portfolio (60-percent large U.S. stocks and 40-percent U.S. intermediate bonds). The 40/60 portfolio is 40-percent large U.S. stocks and 60-percent U.S. intermediate bonds. Annual rebalancing was assumed, but taxes and inflation were not taken into account.

Achieving portfolio "durability" during retirement (when money is being systematically withdrawn) requires the use of a wide variety of assets—including real estate and commodities. To some, this may represent a departure from conventional wisdom. However, the results of the equally weighted seven-asset portfolio compared to the results of a conventional portfolio reveal the importance of creating sufficient portfolio diversity during the post-retirement distribution period.

An equally weighted, multi-asset portfolio had significantly better performance during retirement (meaning that your money would last longer) compared to a 60/40 or 40/60 portfolio. The ending balance in the multi-asset portfolio was roughly *$10 million larger* than the 60/40 and 40/60 portfolios over this specific 39-year period.

The annual year-to-year account balances for all three distribution portfolios are shown in the graph on page 181. The equally weighted, annually rebalanced multi-asset portfolio demonstrates a significant performance advantage during the distribution phase in comparison to a standard 60/40 and 40/60 portfolio.

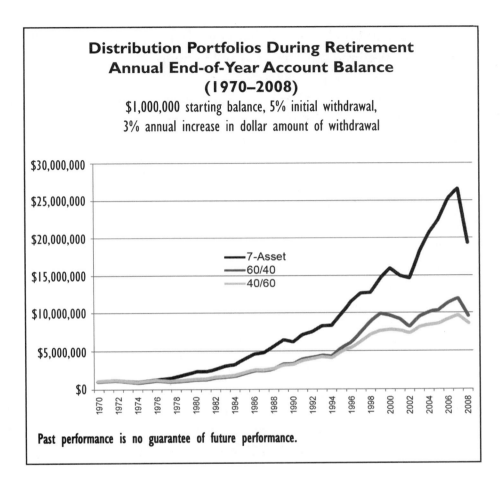

Distribution Portfolios During Retirement
Annual End-of-Year Account Balance
(1970–2008)
$1,000,000 starting balance, 5% initial withdrawal,
3% annual increase in dollar amount of withdrawal

Past performance is no guarantee of future performance.

The key takeaway is that the durability—in other words, the success—of an investment portfolio during retirement requires that a variety of assets be included in the mix.

Where Cash Is King

Though cash alone cannot drive a successful retirement income strategy, it can play an important role in insulating your portfolio from the ups and downs of the market and helping to offset the inherent disadvantages of reverse dollar cost averaging. The key thing you try to avoid during retirement is having to sell holdings during a depressed market. One simple way to achieve that is to establish two investment accounts. The first account would constitute your long-term diversified portfolio with a mix similar to the seven-asset strategy described earlier. This is the money that will keep pace with inflation and ensure a life-time income. The second account supports your day-to-day living expenses. It might represent 10 percent of your overall portfolio, or the amount of liquid assets you would expect to need over the next two years. This second account would be invested in money market accounts, CDs, and short-term bonds—investments that are extremely unlikely to lose value and are always available for withdrawal.

This approach allows your investment account to stay invested through up and down markets, and helps remove much of the fear and uncertainty of today's volatile markets. The day-to-day account can be replenished and maintained by funneling interest and capital gain distributions from the investment account and, when necessary, by strategically liquidating assets. Think of it as a very large checking account that you don't need to worry about. And by not having to worry about your day-to-day needs, you'll be less likely to fret or rejoice over each day's paper loss/gain in your investment account. And that, in a nutshell, is the ultimate goal of your Nest Egg Game Plan.

Chapter 12

I NSURED:
Protecting Your Life, Health, and Money

Peace of mind is a key component of your Nest Egg Game Plan, and it can be enhanced with the judicious use of insurance products. But that peace of mind can come with a high cost if you fall victim to the sales pitches of commission-based financial planners. Make sure you always understand what you're buying, what you're getting in return, and how the various alternatives compare.

Insurance products come in two primary forms: those that protect your assets and those that are supposed to enhance your assets. We say "supposed to enhance" because there is a lot of chicanery hidden below the surface of many asset-enhancing insurance products. You need to know what to ask and what to look for.

We'll quickly review the asset-protection variety of insurance. Many of these are products you've been using for your entire adult life, and their need does not necessarily disappear at retirement. What does change at retirement, however, is how you access and pay for this insurance protection. Most workers depend on employer-provided (and usually employer-subsidized) coverage for their life, health, and disability insurance needs. At retirement the burden falls solidly on your shoulders, and you'll likely suffer a severe case of "sticker shock" as you seek to purchase this insurance protection on your own.

Asset-Protection Insurance

The two forms of insurance that you absolutely must own are health insurance and liability/property insurance.

Health Insurance

The cost of medical care in the United States has skyrocketed, and health insurance premiums have risen at an equally frenetic pace. In researching this book, we came across estimates ranging from $200,000 to $500,000 as the amount a couple would spend on healthcare-related costs during retirement. We include that number not to scare you but to point out that healthcare costs will likely constitute your single largest expense in retirement and to ensure that Your Nest Egg Game Plan appropriately reflects this expenditure. Retirees who are 65 or older are eligible for Medicare, and that is the best primary insurance option for most people. Medicare by itself, however, will not cover all of your healthcare expenses and, as a result, most retirees opt for one of the many Medicare supplement packages. Because health insurance has so many variables, we can't make any hard and fast recommendations other than to make sure your coverage is always current and to do your homework before signing on any dotted line. (Note: Short-term and long-term disability coverage is also a type of health-related insurance. However, because disability insurance is designed to replace your earned income if you're unable to work due to injury or illness, it is no longer needed after retirement.)

Property and Liability Insurance

This is the second requisite and includes insurance on your home (including furnishings and valuables), automobile, boat, RV, motorcycle, and any other personal property of significant value. Just as important, but often overlooked, is the need for a "personal umbrella insurance" policy. This relatively low-cost insurance policy protects you, your family, and your estate against potentially catastrophic financial events. Examples would include being involved in a major car accident and causing damages in excess of your car insurance limits or having someone slip and fall in your yard and winning a multi-million-dollar lawsuit. In each of these cases a personal umbrella policy could save the day by providing insurance coverage well beyond the limits of your primary auto or homeowner's policy.

· · · ·

Once you've taken care of your health and property insurance needs, you start getting into a gray area. If you talk to 10 different financial planners you're likely to hear 10 different views and recommendations about your need for life insurance and long-term care insurance. Because life insurance falls into both the asset-protection and asset-enhancement categories, we'll discuss it in more detail in the stand-alone section that follows. Long-term care insurance, however, is solely an asset-protection product, but, despite its single-purpose design, it is among the most complicated, confusing, and expensive financial products ever created.

The rationale behind long-term care insurance (LTC) is simple: The average cost of a nursing home is about $250 a day, $7,500 a month, and $90,000 a year. The average nursing home stay lasts two years, and, with medical science keeping us alive despite the ravages of cancer, Alzheimer's disease, and heart disease, it is likely that ever-larger percentages of retirees will spend ever-longer periods of time in a nursing home. The numbers are scary, and the idea of spending your last days in a nursing home is particularly disconcerting. The insurance industry thrives in that not-so-sweet spot between scary and disconcerting, and that's what led to the relatively recent introduction of LTC insurance.

LTC insurance typically kicks in when the policyholder suffers from a chronic condition and requires assistance with at least two of the basic tasks of day-to-day living (for example, eating, dressing, bathing, transferring from bed to chair, using the toilet, and remaining continent). "Chronic" means that the condition extends beyond 90 days. Individuals who suffer from serious cognitive impairment due to dementia or Alzheimer's would also qualify for LTC payments. LTC policies typically cover the expenses of nursing homes and assisted-living facilities, but some will also pay for adult daycare or in-home care.

As with all insurance policies, you have to read the fine print. Some LTC policies exclude preexisting conditions or explicitly exclude specific conditions such as Alzheimer's disease. Some LTC policies begin paying immediately, whereas others have an "elimination" or waiting period of 30, 60, or 90 days. The elimination period works like the deductible on a car insurance policy: the higher the deductible (and the longer elimination period), the lower the premium. In addition, LTC payments do not continue forever; they typically have a specific duration (three to five years is most common) and/or a maximum dollar-amount payout.

The biggest drawback to LTC insurance is the cost. Most middle-income individuals and couples cannot afford the premiums. A typical 55-year-old would pay between $1,000 and $4,000 a year for a policy that provides a $150-per-day benefit for three years. The cost would double if the individual purchasing the policy was 65 years old; and if you try to buy coverage when you're in your 70s, you'd be facing annual premiums in the $10,000 to $15,000 range. If there are any health issues present, you probably won't be able to buy insurance at any price.

The decision to buy LTC insurance is deeply personal and complex. It would be impossible to make any broad recommendations. Many people like the comfort of knowing the benefit will be there when they need it; others believe it makes more sense to self-insure. Before deciding, consult with an LTC specialist as opposed to an insurance generalist.

Life Insurance

People tend to regard life insurance in two strikingly different ways: a panacea-like solution for virtually every financial situation or a shell-game scourge that benefits the insurance company and the salesman far more than the consumer. Neither viewpoint is totally true or totally false, but both reflect the financial industry's long-held adage that "life insurance is sold, not bought." That somewhat cynical belief means people need to be "educated" about the myriad benefits of life insurance before they will willingly sign on the dotted line.

Now before we get too far down the jaded path, let's separate life insurance into two camps. The first is pure life insurance—typically called "term life insurance"—that looks and acts just like your homeowner's or auto insurance. This is true "asset protection" insurance. You pay an annual premium for a set period of time and receive a set death benefit. Term life insurance is very inexpensive and is an absolute necessity for anyone with dependents and earned income. Young people in their 30s can buy a million dollars worth of term insurance for just a few hundred dollars a year. Most working people purchase term insurance through their employer, in amounts equal to one to five times their annual income. And despite the industry's "sold not bought" adage, people do proactively seek out term life insurance to protect their family in the case of premature death. Term insurance is easy to understand. You know exactly what you're paying and what you're getting in return.

Term insurance, however, is not particularly profitable for insurance companies or insurance salespeople. Think of it in terms of buying a car. Term insurance is like the stripped-down model with manual transmission and no air conditioning. It's unlikely the car dealer will even have a base model on the lot; even if he does, he will nonetheless direct your attention to the benefits of the upscale model with lots of bells and whistles—"all for only X dollars more a month." The base model is a loss leader; the real money is made with the leather trim, the Bose audio system, and the sunroof. The salesman, the car dealer, and the manufacturer all make higher commissions and higher profits on a "loaded" car.

The loaded version of life insurance is called cash-value insurance— also known as whole life, universal life, or variable life—and falls into the asset-enhancing category. Cash-value insurance combines the insurance protection of term life with a savings component. It's important that you view cash-value insurance in those terms because when you buy cash-value life insurance you're actually buying term insurance (sometimes explicitly in the case of universal or variable life) and investing in an "accumulation account." The accumulation account will grow over time based on interest rates or the performance of the stock market. The accumulation account is what drives the huge difference in premiums between term and cash-value insurance. Cash-value policies often cost 10 to 15 times more than term insurance. Insurance companies will argue that cash-value policies are permanent and provide substantial benefits over and above the core insurance protection. They'll show you that the money you spend on term insurance is gone once the policy lapses, whereas cash-value insurance will pay back all or part of what you paid in premiums. And they'll show you a mountain of hypothetical charts demonstrating how cash-value life insurance can help you save more, earn more, and leave more to your heirs. Few of us are able to make sense of these tables and charts, and even fewer can accurately compare these hypothetical illustrations to alternative products or strategies. In truth, the insurance industry counts on that. The product is confusing, and the paperwork provides a shield of credibility and mathematical precision.

From our perspective, the vast majority of retirees do not need any life insurance coverage because their death will not constitute a financial burden for their family. The children are grown and out on their own. If the retiree has a pension or annuity, he should have chosen the joint-life payout option so the surviving spouse continues to receive monthly income. Remember: Life insurance is designed to replace income that will disappear upon the death of the insured. It's not designed to create wealth or help heal the emotional pain of having a loved one die.

There are two retirement-centric usages for cash-value insurance that are often written about and touted by insurance salesmen: pension maximization and estate planning. Here's a brief introduction to both:

> ⊳ **Pension maximization:** This strategy is designed to appeal to individuals who receive a lifetime pension or annuity payout. When it's time for the payout to begin, the pensioner or annuitant must decide on a single-life or joint-and-survivor structure. Using round numbers, the single-life option might pay $2,500 a month versus $2,000 for the joint-and-survivor option. The single-life option, however, ceases payment upon the death of the pensioner or annuitant. The joint-and-survivor option continues payments until both parties have died. The pension maximization concept allows you to take the higher single-life benefit and "invest" the $500 monthly difference in a life insurance policy. The idea is that, if the pensioner dies, the surviving spouse will receive a death benefit large enough to generate income equal to or greater than the joint-and-survivor option. At first blush, it sounds like a decent idea,

but upon closer examination there are so many holes in the rationale and so many variables at play that the idea of pension maximization has more in common with a Las Vegas crapshoot than a guaranteed insurance product. If someone touts pension maximization, make sure you walk away at maximum speed.

▹ **Estate planning:** If you count yourself among the truly affluent, then life insurance might make sense as a wealth transfer tool, but, as with pension maximization, you need to look at the numbers and weigh the alternatives very closely. When used as part of an estate planning strategy, life insurance usually provides liquidity to pay the taxes and administrative costs associated with a major inheritance. This is especially important when the bulk of the estate value is tied up in illiquid assets such as a business, real estate, art-work, or heirloom jewelry. The proceeds from the life in-surance policy can pay the taxes due without having to sell the estate's assets. Life insurance can also be used to divide an estate equitably. For example, the owner of a business worth $1 million might leave the entire business to one child and provide $1 million to another child in the form of a life insurance policy.

Recently, a new use for life insurance has been introduced that may be of interest to retirees in need of extra income. Called "life insurance settlements," the process involves the ownership transfer of a life insurance policy to a third party in exchange for financial com-pensation. Essentially, the third party buys the life insurance policy for an amount less than the death benefit. The retiree who sells the policy receives an immediate lump sum; the party buying the policy will col-lect the full amount of the death benefit when the originally policy-holder dies. The settlement amount varies greatly depending on the age and health of the original policyholder. The younger and healthier you are, the less you'll receive as compensation. There is also a specific form of life insurance settlement—called viatical settlements—aimed at the terminally ill. Though there are some unsavory aspects of the life settlement and viatical settlement concepts, they can provide a helpful solution in certain circumstances. Before committing to a life settlement program make sure you consult with an attorney and accountant to consider any legal and tax ramifications.

Annuities

Many people have a knee-jerk reaction against annuities—and with some justification. Annuities, especially the variable and equity-indexed varieties, are the most oversold and blatantly misrepresented products offered by the financial services industry. Annuities are also complicated and difficult for the layman to understand. This complexity tends to increase the marketing costs for annuities—costs that ultimately get passed on to the consumer in terms of higher fees. Nonetheless, annuities can play an important role in your Nest Egg Game Plan as long as you choose wisely.

Annuities come in a variety of forms and we'll examine each of them in the sections that follow.

Deferred Annuities

Deferred annuities are offered in fixed and variable form. You invest a lump sum or a series of periodic payments into a deferred annuity and your investment grows tax-deferred, similar to what happens inside a 401(k) or IRA. You pay tax only on the earnings and only when money is withdrawn. Unlike a 401(k) or IRA, you invest in a deferred annuity with post-tax dollars. As a result, most people should fully fund their 401(k) and IRA before even considering investing in an annuity.

Deferred fixed annuities look a lot like CDs and savings accounts with a life insurance wrapper. They typically pay a fixed rate of return based on prevailing interest rates. Oftentimes, they include a "teaser" introductory rate that is higher than current interest rates and is guaranteed for a specified amount of time (usually two to five years). After that introductory period, the interest rate earned will vary based on current rates. Deferred fixed annuities are fairly simple products, but it pays to shop around. Keep in mind that the guarantees offered by these products are backed by the underlying insurance company, so limit your selection to top-rated insurers.

Deferred variable annuities are a whole different ballgame. Although they may look like a selection of mutual funds inside a life insurance wrapper, they are far more complicated than that. Unlike fixed annuities that offer a guaranteed rate of return, the performance of a variable annuity depends on how good a job you do in selecting the mutual funds you want to invest in and how well the portfolio managers of those mutual funds do when investing your money.

Variable annuities are also heavily laden with expenses. The average variable annuity charges fees of about 1.25 percent. When you consider that those fees are on top of the management fees charged by the underlying mutual funds, your all-in expense will almost always exceed 2 percent and will occasionally top the 3-percent level. That is a big hurdle to make up and explains why we, and many industry observers, recommend against variable annuities. The exception would be the usage of low-cost variable annuities from companies like Vanguard or TIAA-CREF or the new breed of variable annuities designed for fee-based advisors that charge a flat fee of $20 per month in lieu of traditional built-in "mortality" and "administrative" expenses.

Equity-Indexed Annuities

Equity-indexed annuities are truly evil products that serve no purpose other than to enrich the insurance companies and salesmen who foist them on innocent and gullible consumers (especially seniors). In a statement issued in June 2008, Christopher Cox, then-chairman of the Securities and Exchange Commission, discussed federal efforts to expose "the abusive sales practices often used to promote equity-indexed annuities to older investors for whom they are unsuitable" (available at *www.sec.gov/news/speech/2008/spch062508cc_annuity.htm*). He also pointed to the results of a national survey regarding equity-indexed annuities that "revealed a landscape littered with slick schemes and broken dreams that has been devastating to the victims and their families."

Rather than wasting time describing the workings of these products—for example, the double-digit commissions and surrender charges that can total 15 percent to 20 percent of the amount invested—suffice it to say that you should eliminate them from your vocabulary and your portfolio.

Income Annuities

Income annuities (also called payout annuities) are the closest thing individual investors can get to the benefits and peace of mind of a traditional pension plan. In exchange for a lump-sum investment, the insurance company behind the annuity guarantees to provide lifetime income, in monthly installments, no matter how long you live. Because this guarantee is only as strong as the company making the guarantee, limit your choices to insurers with the highest ratings and strongest reputation. You'll always be able to find lower-tier insurers offering higher rates of return, but, if you're truly buying peace of mind, you'll want to stick with the best. And as with all financial products, the built-in (and often hidden) expenses of income annuities have a significant impact on your rate of return so give close consideration to the low-cost annuities offered by firms like Vanguard, Fidelity, and TIAA-CREF.

Income annuities come in different varieties: immediate or deferred, fixed or variable, single or joint.

As their name implies, immediate annuities begin generating monthly income within 30 days of the initial investment. These are typically purchased at retirement or shortly thereafter. With deferred annuities, on the other hand, your initial investment grows inside the product on a tax-deferred basis until payouts begin (usually on a pre-determined date).

Fixed income annuities pay a level amount every month, though some contracts do provide for inflationary increases. Variable income annuities are quite a different animal. Their monthly payments are adjusted annually to reflect the performance of the underlying mutual funds (which reflect the performance of the stock and bond markets). This means your income will likely fluctuate dramatically, thereby defeating the purpose of buying an income annuity in the first place.

Income annuities can be purchased and issued either for the life of an individual or a couple (in other words, a joint-life annuity). Because income annuity payments are based on life expectancy, all things being equal, a single-life annuity will have a higher monthly payout than a joint-life annuity.

One of the unique features of annuities is the way distributions are treated for tax purposes. Using its own life expectancy tables, the IRS estimates how many monthly annuity payments you're likely to receive (in other words, when the IRS expects you to die) and calculates an "exclusion ratio." The exclusion ratio determines how much of each monthly payment is considered a "return of principal" and thus not subject to income tax. It would not be unusual for only one-half of an annuity's monthly payout to be taxable.

A fixed immediate annuity can play an important role in constructing Your Nest Egg Game Plan. It provides guarantees that are unavailable elsewhere and can significantly lower the risk profile of your overall investment portfolio. Other than retirees who already have a traditional pension plan, most people would be well served to invest a portion of their savings (perhaps 25 percent) in a fixed income annuity.

As valuable as fixed immediate annuities are in a well-designed retirement income plan, a relatively small number of people choose them. Part of the resistance is the negative knee-jerk reaction we mentioned earlier, but other considerations also come into play. Most 401(k) plans pay out a lump-sum benefit at retirement. This money is typically rolled into an IRA and invested in a variety of stocks, bonds, and cash equivalents. The benefactors of those lump sums like having a pile of money they can call their own and they want to keep it for their own. They view it as a safety net but, in truth, they are undermining their long-term safety. Very few people understand the risk of outliving their lump-sum resources, they don't understand the mechanics of managing an income stream, and they don't appreciate the higher standard of living and peace of mind that a guaranteed annuity can deliver. So before you rule out including a fixed immediate annuity in your retirement plan, do some homework. You'll be glad you did.

Longevity Insurance

The biggest fear retirees face is outliving their assets. Leaving aside the lifetime income streams provided by traditional pensions and Social Security, the only available product that could truly guarantee lifetime income was the immediate fixed annuity discussed in the previous section. Recognizing retirees' need for more options, however, the insurance industry recently introduced a variation on the fixed annuity that could appeal to a certain group of investors. The product is called "longevity insurance" or a longevity annuity, and it looks a lot like a deferred fixed annuity with a couple of key differences.

But first let's look at the similarities. Deferred fixed annuities and longevity annuities are both funded with a lump-sum investment and are designed to begin predetermined payouts at a predetermined date in the future. Let's assume a 65-year-old invests $100,000 in both types of products and wants to begin collecting income at age 85. Using ballpark figures (because exact payout amounts change daily based on prevailing interest rates), the deferred fixed annuity would pay $1,400 per month beginning at age 85, whereas the longevity annuity would pay $7,000 per month. The payout difference is strikingly large due to the critical differences between the two products:

- ⯈ Deferred annuities offer a death benefit. If you die before payouts begin, your heirs will receive your principal and accumulated earnings. If you die before payouts begin on a longevity annuity, you and your heirs get nothing. The insurance company keeps it all.

- ⯈ Deferred annuities come with a minimum guaranteed return on your investment during the deferral period, but they may earn a higher return depending on market conditions. With longevity annuities, on the other hand, your implied rate-of-return is fixed regardless of what happens to interest rates during the 20-year deferral period.

- ⯈ Deferred annuities also offer more flexibility in terms of partial or total withdrawals from the product. With longevity annuities you're locked in for life.

Being "locked in for life" is a huge disadvantage if you don't live long enough to collect income from the product, but it is a huge advantage if you live well beyond the payout date. Essentially, you're betting against the insurance company, and the odds are stacked against you. The trade-off is that the cost is miniscule compared to the potential benefit. That's because you're being paid from the proceeds of the insurance company's other customers who didn't live long enough to collect a dime of their investment.

Despite their inherent drawbacks, longevity annuities can be a good choice for a small portion of your investment portfolio if—and it's an especially important "if"—you're in good health and descended from a long line of centagenarians. The comfort of knowing that extra income will be there just when you're most likely to need it for healthcare or assisted-living expenses can far outweigh the cost and inflexibility.

Chapter 13

I MMEDIATE:
Ensuring Liquidity When You Need It

Stuff happens in life—whether you're working or retired—and your Nest Egg Game Plan needs to reflect the immediate cash flow needs of car repairs, home improvements, medical emergencies, or even fun stuff like spur-of-the-moment vacations. Of course, there's a delicate balance between having immediate access to funds and giving up the generally higher returns that less-liquid, longer-term investments offer. The trade-off is between security and growth; safety and risk; guarantees and volatility. Like all trade-offs, this one works best when you understand the various alternatives and choose the one that works best for you.

Take Distributions in Cash

One of the key tenets of investing during your wealth-accumulation years is the idea of reinvesting dividends and distributions. Over time this forced dollar-cost averaging can substantially boost your returns. During retirement, however, your needs are quite different, so you should ensure that all distributions are paid in cash rather than reinvesting them in the underlying fund or security. By doing so, you can generate income without having to sell assets or use the cash as part of a rebalancing strategy. And because taxation is the same whether you reinvest or take distributions in cash, this approach offers the additional benefit of tax efficiency when used in lieu of selling assets.

Rebalance to Help Ensure Liquidity

Rebalancing is a systematic process of reallocating the assets within a portfolio in order to keep each asset's weighting in line with a predetermined percentage. For example, if a portfolio utilizes five different asset classes and the goal is for each to represent 20 percent of the total value, the portfolio will need to be rebalanced periodically to maintain the equal weighting. This is because each asset class will experience differing returns.

After one year (or whatever rebalancing time frame is selected) the best-performing asset will represent more than 20 percent of the portfolio while the worst-performing asset will represent less than 20 percent. The process of rebalancing will require that some portion of the best performing asset be sold and the proceeds used to purchase more of the worst performing asset. Tax efficiency can be improved if new cash inflows are used to accomplish the needed rebalance, especially if done within a taxable account.

Rebalancing takes some time and thought, but it rewards you with markedly improved performance. Here's how it works. Let's assume you held a seven-asset portfolio over the 39-year period from January 1, 1970, to December 31, 2008. The asset classes include large-cap U.S. stocks, small-cap U.S. stocks, international stocks, U.S. intermediate-term bonds, cash, real estate, and commodities. The

impact of rebalancing was studied by investing a total of $10,000 in
the seven-asset portfolio on January 1, 1970, with each asset receiving one-seventh of the total investment, or $1,428. Using that same
starting point, we simulated two portfolios: one that was annually rebalanced back to the one-seventh weighting, and one that represented a
static buy-and-hold portfolio with no rebalancing over the entire 39-
year period. As you can see in "The Long Run" graphic, the annually
rebalanced portfolio began to significantly outperform by 1990, and
by the end of the 39-year period it was worth $114,000 more than the
buy-and-hold portfolio.

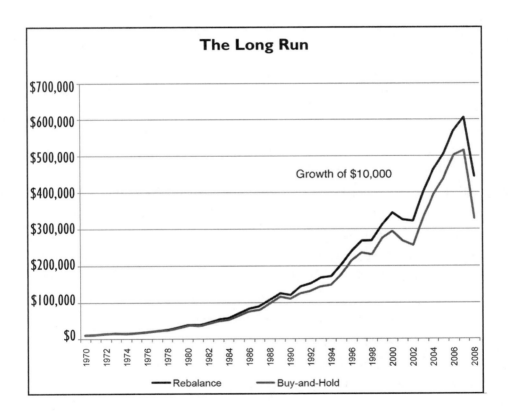

The obvious question is: What does this have to do with the concepts of immediacy and liquidity? The answer is in the "Total Ending Balances" chart.

Total Ending Balances
January 1, 1970 to December 31, 2008

$1,428 starting balance in each of the 7 assets	Large U.S. Equity	Small U.S. Equity	Non-U.S. Equity	U.S Bonds	Cash	REIT	Commodities	Total Portfolio Value (Growth of $10,000)
Annually Rebalanced	54,461	57,236	48,946	95,462	87,751	52,559	46,257	442,671
Buy-and-Hold	48,784	64,118	40,716	30,090	14,748	73,296	57,117	328,868

Take a look at the massive difference in the "Cash" column. The annually rebalanced portfolio had a final account balance of nearly $88,000 in cash, whereas the buy-and-hold portfolio had just under $15,000. The difference results from the fact that, over long time periods, assets that generate lower returns, such as bonds and cash, will be unable to produce account balances that keep pace with higher returning equity-based assets. Why does this matter? Three words: *unexpected liquidity needs.* Maintaining one or more asset classes that can provide immediate liquidity is vitally important, as evidenced by the carnage experienced in 2008.

So rebalancing accomplishes two key goals. It delivers superior performance and, by diverting excess equity returns to the fixed income components of the portfolio (cash and bonds), the gains are preserved in a fixed income "lockbox." As investors age, this notion of a secure lockbox becomes very appealing, and achieving it does not require that a portfolio be moved entirely to cash or bonds. Rather, systematic rebalancing can go a long way in creating a safe haven for today and tomorrow.

Ladder Your Bond Portfolio

Bond laddering has advantages for all investors but is especially valuable for retirees. At its core, a bond ladder helps match cash flow with future income needs, while providing some protection against interest-rate risk (that is, if interest rates rise you'll be able to take the proceeds from the maturing bonds and invest in new higher-yielding bonds) as well as reinvestment risk (in other words, your longer-term bonds will provide a hedge against falling interest rates). Here's how it works.

First off, bond laddering only works with individual bonds. It does not work with bond mutual funds or ETFs. That's because bonds have a set maturity whereas bond funds and ETFs do not. You could, on the other hand, purchase bond funds and ETFs and sell shares as needed to raise cash, but that process can be expensive and inefficient from both a transaction cost and taxation perspective.

So the bond ladder begins with the purchase of a series of bonds—typically three to 10 different issues—with staggered maturity dates. For simplicity sake, we'll use a three-bond example as illustrated in the accompanying graphic. At the beginning of the first year, you'll purchase three bonds with equal face amounts of $20,000. Bond A has a one-year maturity, Bond B a two-year maturity, and Bond C a three-year maturity. As you extend the maturity, the yields on the bonds increase. (Note: There are instances when longer durations do not deliver higher yields, resulting in an inverted yield curve, but that is the exception, not the norm.) At the end of Year 1, Bond A matures and you receive your $20,000 principal plus interest. Bonds B and C are still working for you. You then use the proceeds from Bond A and purchase Bond D with a three-year maturity. At the end of Year 2, Bond B matures and you use its proceeds to purchase Bond E with a three-year maturity. The process continues in Years 3 and beyond.

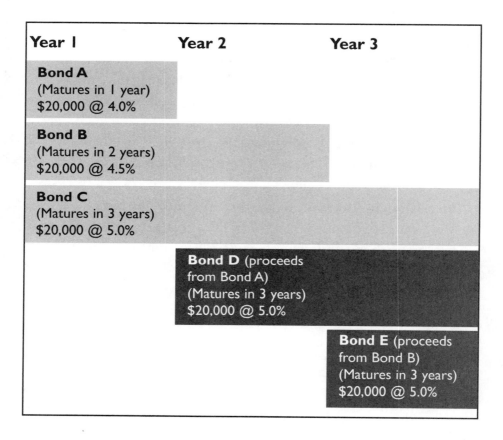

A similar ladder can be built with any sequence of maturities. The common element is that you replace each matured bond with a bond equal to the longest maturity in the portfolio. In our example, every newly purchased bond has a three-year maturity. If you were building a five-bond ladder with maturities of two, four, six, eight, and 10 years, then each newly purchased bond would have a 10-year maturity.

The downside to a bond ladder is that your overall return might be lower than if you invested all of your money ($60,000 in the previously illustrated example) in a single longer-term bond. So instead of having $20,000 in Bond A yielding 4 percent and another $20,000 in Bond B earning 4.5 percent, you would have all $60,000 in Bond C working for you at 5 percent. The drawback of that all-in-one approach is that you're essentially illiquid for three years. (In truth, bonds can be bought and sold just like stocks, but the trading process is much less efficient and much more expensive. Accordingly, the average investor should only purchase bonds with the expectation of holding them to maturity.)

Keep Your Home Equity Line of Credit Option

When home equity lines of credit were first introduced, they were used primarily for home improvements and other big-ticket expenditures. As people became more comfortable with the notion of borrowing against the equity in their homes, especially as real estate values soared, home equity lines were increasingly viewed as a cash management tool, a source of instant liquidity, and an alternative to the discipline of "saving for a rainy day." Banks loved the concept and wooed homeowners with low teaser rates and no-cost closings. In retrospect, of course, we all know how the mortgage business self-destructed with the sub-prime debacle of 2007–2008 and the demise of once-glorious banks like Washington Mutual and Wachovia. Notwithstanding the fact that some banks and some homeowners abused the privilege, a home equity line of credit can serve as a short-term liquidity solution—with major emphasis on "short-term." Retirement is not the time to be taking on additional debt. The burden of paying down debt serves only to lessen your standard of living and add stress to what should be as stress-free a time as possible. If you do have a home equity line of credit, keep it on the sidelines until a serious need arises. And promise yourself to pay it off completely within 12 to 18 months.

Safeguard Your Nest Egg Liquidity With a Reserve Fund

Anyone who was retired during the market meltdown of 2007–2008 suffered many long and sleepless nights. Despite all the back-testing and Monte Carlo simulations that assured them they could annually withdraw 4 percent or 5 percent of their portfolio and never run out of money, the ballgame was now dramatically changed. Even conservative investors experienced losses of 20 percent or more, as normally safe-haven investments like bonds tumbled along with the stock market. There truly was no place to hide, and investors who were withdrawing money to cover day-to-day expenses were being hit with a double whammy: declining prices and reverse dollar-cost averaging.

This concept of reverse dollar-cost averaging is critically important but often ignored or not understood. During our capital-accumulation years, the benefits of dollar-cost averaging were a constant refrain. "Buy more when prices are low" and view every market dip as "a buying opportunity." The opposite is true during the income-generation life stage. During bear markets, income investors are forced to sell more shares at low prices, and, once sold, even if the underlying security increases in price, your loss is permanent with no possibility of recovery. A key element of your Nest Egg Game Plan is to avoid having to sell holdings during a depressed market.

The only 100-percent safe investments are cash and cash equivalents like money market funds, Treasury bills, CDs, and short-term bonds. And although you might be tempted to dump all your savings into a cash account to protect yourself from the ravages of a bear market, it would be a mistake. Cash alone cannot drive a successful retirement income strategy. Cash investments struggle to simply keep pace with inflation and would never be able to support a 4-percent or 5-percent income-generation strategy. Notwithstanding that reality, cash can and should play an important role in insulating your portfolio from the ups and downs of the market and offsetting the inherent disadvantages of reverse dollar-cost averaging. One simple way to achieve that is to establish two investment accounts. The first account would constitute your long-term diversified portfolio with a mix similar to the seven-asset strategy described previously. This is the money that will keep pace with inflation and ensure a lifetime income, and might represent 90 percent of your portfolio. The second account supports your day-to-day living expenses. It might represent 10 percent of your overall portfolio or the amount of liquid assets you would expect to need over the next two years. This second account would be invested in money market accounts, CDs, and short-term bonds—investments that are extremely unlikely to lose value and are always available for withdrawal.

Shown in the "Growth of $10,000" graph that follows on page 206 is an 80/20 portfolio ($8,000 invested in the seven-asset model and $2,000 invested in a cash reserve account) compared against a 60/40 portfolio ($6,000 invested in large U.S. stocks and $4,000 invested in U.S. intermediate term bonds).

The dark gray bars represent the growth of the $8,000 invested in the seven-asset portion of the portfolio; the light gray bars on top represent the steady growth of $2,000 invested in cash. The cash account slowly increased each year and was always available for liquidity needs. The black line represents the growth of $10,000 invested in a typical 60/40 portfolio. The 80/20 portfolio had a higher year-end balance 82 percent of the time—plus, it had a steady cash component that never had a negative return in any of the 39 years from 1970 to 2008. Of course, the growth potential of cash is far less than a stock and bond portfolio (either the seven-asset or 60/40 portfolio), but the important purpose of the cash component is liquidity. This comparison provides further evidence that adding an extra cash component to an already-diversified seven-asset portfolio does not degrade the overall performance. Rather, it adds an important additional dimension of security and safety.

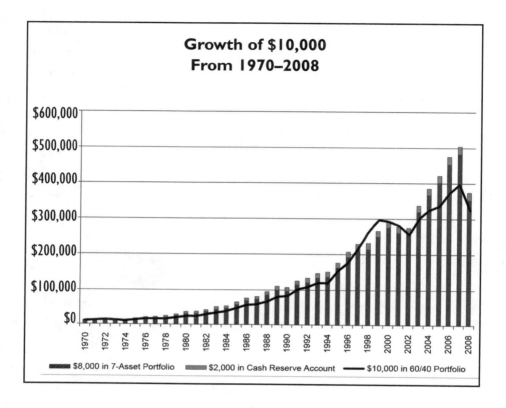

This approach allows your investment account to stay invested through up and down markets and helps remove much of the fear and uncertainty of today's volatile markets. The day-to-day account can be replenished and maintained by funneling interest and capital gain distributions from the investment account and, when necessary, by strategically liquidating assets. Think of it as a very large checking account that you don't have to worry about. By not needing to worry about your immediate day-to-day needs, you'll be less likely to fret or rejoice over each day's paper loss/gain in your investment account. This two-account approach provides the ultimate in liquidity, flexibility, and peace of mind—and that, in a nutshell, is the ultimate goal of your Nest Egg Game Plan.

Be an Optimist, but Consider Worst-Case Scenarios

When most people think about and plan for the future, they focus on the good stuff. That's appropriate because no one should go through life as a "Debbie Downer" perpetual pessimist. On the flipside, however, retirement is one of those times when envisioning worst-case scenarios can be beneficial in avoiding them.

Think about your Nest Egg Game Plan as a business with you as the CEO. Like every business, yours should include a "disaster recovery" plan and contingency plans. If a crisis hits, you don't want to be forced to make decisions on the fly. Instead, you'll want to be able to respond with corrective action immediately and aggressively to ensure that the crisis is contained and does as little permanent damage as possible.

Consider these types of what-if scenarios as you develop your personal disaster recovery plan:

▷ What if you had to liquidate and spend 20 percent of your remaining assets in the second year of your Nest Egg Pension Plan? What if that happened in the fifth or 10th year? What would the rest of your retirement years look like? What changes would you have to make to your lifestyle or legacy plans?

▷ What if inflation returns to the double-digit levels of the 1980s and your investments do not keep pace? Where will the extra money needed to maintain your planned lifestyle come from?

▷ What if interest rates plummeted and your fixed income investments yielded a negative amount after accounting for taxes and inflation?

▷ What if your spouse dies before you? Will your financial situation change?

▷ What if you die before your spouse? Will he or she be able to live comfortably? Will his or her lifestyle need to change?

> ⊳ What if you're counting on part-time work to supplement your income during the early years of retirement and, due to illness or injury, that is no longer an option?

> ⊳ What if your income-generation model illustrates a 90-percent success rate for never running out of money—and you fall into the 10-percent failure rate?

Contemplating these kinds of questions and the large-scale issues they raise will help you consider the implications of every decision you make and the trade-offs you are willing to accept. Ignoring them can lock you into a game plan that is unsustainable, unsatisfactory, and, ultimately, unsuccessful.

Chapter 14

I NEVITABLE:
Preparing for Your Departure

All good things come to an end—including each of our lives. And while death is hardly something to look forward to, it must be considered and prepared for. Indeed, a well-crafted Nest Egg Game Plan must include estate planning as a critical component.

The first question every retiree must answer—and this should happen long before death is considered imminent—is: How much money do you want to die with? If you could know the exact moment you were going to die, would you want to have spent your last penny on that morning's breakfast? Or would you prefer to leave an inheritance—modest or sizeable—to your heirs or to a favorite charity? The answers to those questions will have major impact on how you manage your retirement assets and how you monitor your "number" at each annual review. And as you consider this, keep in mind that most income-generation simulations focus on the "dying broke" scenario—and must be substantially reconfigured to provide simulations that include an inheritance.

Determining whether you want to die poor or flush with cash also has significant implications for structuring your estate plan. Having a will is the most basic step you can take, but it is not the only one. Depending on your asset base, a trust may also be in your best interests. An attorney and accountant should be consulted to review the various types of trusts and their respective effectiveness.

It is also important to recognize that all assets are not created equal in the eyes of the IRS—especially at death. Although some assets can be passed on tax-free, some will be taxed at ordinary income tax rates, and others will be taxed at the long-term capital gains tax rate. With the continually changing U.S. tax code, it's hard to predict which investment vehicles and strategies would be most advantageous, but you should spend some time understanding how the various options compare and relate to each other.

Your Last Will and Testament

As we researched this book one of the most surprising facts we uncovered was that more than half (55 percent to be exact, according to this site: *research.lawyers.com/Majority-of-American-Adults-Remain-Without-Wills.html*) of adult Americans do not have a will. There is no excuse for this glaring omission, because a will represents the cornerstone of your estate plan. It presents a clear road map to how you would like your remaining assets to be distributed among your heirs. A will is also the least-complex legal document you will every encounter. You can simply and inexpensively write your own will, use an online service, or hire an attorney. In order to be legally binding, your will simply needs to satisfy these requirements:

> ⇁ You must be "of sound mind." This is a critical reason to create your will before suffering a cognitive debilitation like dementia or Alzheimer's disease, or before a stroke or other ailment affects your ability to communicate.

▶ The document should be typed.

▶ The document must clearly identify the person making the will and state that it supersedes any previously written wills.

▶ You must sign and date the document.

▶ You need to have two witnesses watch you sign the will and then sign it themselves.

That's really it. The will does not need to be notarized (though doing so could ease the probate process if the witnesses are deceased or cannot be located), filed with any agency, bound, or printed on fancy paper.

In addition to specifying how you want your assets to be divided, your will should appoint an executor. This is a key position empowered with the responsibility to ensure that your wishes, as stated in the will, are carried out. Depending on the size of the estate, the executor may have to manage your finances (for example, pay taxes and bills) during the probate process. Your executor should be a person of the utmost integrity with whom you are entrusting your worldly possessions after you've left this world. In most cases, you should specify a successor executor in the event the primary executor cannot serve.

Keep in mind also that a will can be overridden by other documentation that specifies how you want certain assets to be assigned at your death. For example:

▶ 401(k) retirement accounts automatically get passed on to the spouse unless the spouse has signed a notarized statement waiving his or her rights. Consider this example. You were single, widowed, or divorced when you opened your 401(k) account, and you named a child or sibling as your beneficiary. If you subsequently got married, your new spouse would inherit the assets unless you remembered to have him or her waive this right in front of a notary.

> ▷ Similarly, the beneficiary designation on IRA accounts and life insurance policies take precedence over wishes expressed in a will. Because these initial beneficiary designations often precede death by decades, the donor often forgets what beneficiaries were specified. In today's world of complicated family dynamics, you'll be well served to revisit and update the beneficiary forms of all potentially problematic accounts and assets.

> ▷ Any assets held as "joint tenancy with rights of survivorship" or "tenancy by the entirety" will also change ownership without regard to one's wishes as stated in a will. This type of titling is most common with real estate property and brokerage accounts.

A will reflects your wishes at the time you write it. But things do change in life, and your will cannot update itself automatically. Accordingly, it makes sense to review your will at least every few years to ensure it is current. If, for example, your will specifies two grandchildren to inherit a particular asset and then a third grandchild arrives, if you die before modifying the will the third grandchild will be left out.

Because of these complicating factors, it probably makes sense for most people to consult an attorney when drawing up a will. But as with all elements of your Nest Egg Game Plan, it depends on your comfort factor.

Living Trust

Living trusts have become increasingly popular in recent years, and they can indeed be beneficial in planning your estate. Before creating a living trust, however, make sure to carefully weigh the advantages of a trust versus the time and cost of doing so. A will and a living trust are both designed to accomplish similar objectives—that is, leaving your assets and property to named beneficiaries. The key advantage of a living trust is that this transfer of assets happens outside of probate. That means the transfer can happen faster and more privately with a trust versus a will.

In simplest terms, a living trust involves the legal transfer of property to a trust while you're still alive. Typically, the donor of the property names himself as the trustee. In the case of a shared trust, spouses would typically both serve as the initial trustees. The trustee provides oversight and management of the trust assets during his or her lifetime. At death, the successor trustee (who was named in the original documentation) will manage the assets and distribute them to the named beneficiaries without court intervention.

Living trusts are most appropriate and beneficial to people who have minor children or other dependents with special needs (as the trust can specify legal guardianship), multiple parcels of real property (as these tend to be held up longer in probate) or large estates likely to be subject to estate taxation (as the trust can include some tax-planning provisions).

One final point: Do not decide that you need a living trust based on attending a "free seminar" presented by well-dressed high-pressure salesmen. These types of seminars are designed to scare people into preparing a trust and often lead to sales pitches for life insurance, annuities, and long-term care insurance. If you need a trust, consult your family attorney or ask a trusted friend or family member for a referral.

Gifting: Make a Difference While You're Still Alive

If you've been fortunate enough to accumulate sufficient assets to live comfortably and still expect to have money left over when you die, you may want to consider the merits of a systematic gifting program.

Until recent years, gifting was valued primarily as a means of shifting assets out of one's estate to reduce the tax burden on heirs. With the current estate tax exemption of $3.5 million, however, this need applies only to the wealthiest of Americans. But even without estate tax implications, gifting can provide a deep and long-lasting benefit to most people: the joy of making a difference in a loved one's life and being present to experience that difference firsthand.

For 2009, you can give away up to $13,000 per year to each beneficiary, and your spouse can do the same. (The amount changes annually.) That means couples can give away $26,000 in 2009 to each beneficiary, and there is no limit to the number of beneficiaries receiving gifts. Individuals with large extended families could easily—and legally—give away several hundred thousand dollars a year. This is money that could pay for a grandchild's college tuition, provide a down payment on a house, or fund a startup business.

Gifts are not taxable and don't need to be reported on the beneficiaries' tax returns. As the donor, you only need to file a gift tax form if you exceed the $13,000 limit per beneficiary. If you do exceed the annual gift limit, you will need to use IRS Form 709 to file a federal gift tax return. Amounts in excess of $13,000 are considered "taxable gifts" but, in reality, you won't owe any tax until and unless you exceed the $1 million lifetime gift tax exemption.

Charitable Giving: Make a Difference When You're Gone

Bill Gates, the founder of Microsoft, and his wife, Melinda, are hardly everyday people when it comes to financial resources, but they have become exemplars of the power of charitable giving. Here's how they explain their vision on their Website (*www.gatesfoundation.org/about/Pages/bill-melinda-gates-letter.aspx*):

We created the Gates Foundation in 2000 because we believe in the principle that every human life has equal worth. The life of an impoverished child in a developing country is as precious as the life of a middle-class kid in a developed one. A family struggling to make ends meet in an American inner city matters as much as a family thriving in a safe, suburban neighborhood.

Today, billions of people never even have the chance to live a healthy, productive life. We want to help all people get that opportunity.

Everyone can make a difference during their lifetime and after; and the Federal tax code provides strong incentives to donate to charitable institutions and organizations. At death, any gifts you leave to qualified charitable organizations are exempt from Federal tax.

There are two basic ways to leave money to charity. The simplest is to include the charity in your will and specify the amount of money (or the specific assets) you want to pass on to that organization. This approach keeps the assets completely under your control during your lifetime, and, if something changes prior to your death, you can easily modify your will to exclude or change the charity or modify the amount of money you want to pass along.

A different approach is to create a formal arrangement with the charity during your lifetime and receive an immediate tax benefit. The two most common structures are a Charitable Gift Annuity and a Charitable Remainder Trust.

Charitable Gift Annuity

Similar to an immediate annuity purchased from a life insurance company, a Charitable Gift Annuity is a contract between the donor and the specific charity. In return for a fixed sum of money, the charity promises to provide a lifetime stream of income payments. And as with typical annuities, you can choose the income to last for a single life or the joint life of a couple. At the time of the gift, the donor receives a tax deduction for the full amount of the lump sum. The downside to gift annuities is that their income payments are fixed rather than being tied to inflation. In addition, unlike many insurance annuities, there is no minimum number of payments or return of principal to heirs should the beneficiary die prematurely.

Charitable Remainder Trust

Though more common among wealthy individuals, a Charitable Remainder Trust (CRT) is an especially efficient way to make a sizeable donation and still receive financial benefits during your lifetime. A CRT is an irrevocable gift of money or property to a charity while the donor receives a pre-established income stream for life. At death, the charity receives full ownership of whatever principal or asset value remains. When the CRT is established, the donor receives an income tax deduction equal to the amount of the gift less the present value of the remainder interest that the charity will ultimately receive. (Note: This present value calculation is complicated even by IRS standards, so you should consult an accountant to gain a full understanding of a CRT's tax implications.)

Life Insurance

Life insurance is often discussed as an estate-planning tool, and, though it certainly has some application for some people, the benefits of life insurance are often exaggerated or misrepresented. Now please remember: We're talking about life insurance for older individuals who are retired with no dependents. Life insurance is an absolute necessity for young people with earned income and young children. These individuals need the protection of life insurance to ensure that their dependents can maintain current lifestyles in the event of premature death.

Retired people who are living off assets rather than earned income generally don't need life insurance. That doesn't means they should run out and cash in any life insurance policies they have in force, but they should be very circumspect about purchasing new policies. There are two exceptions to this. Wealthy individuals and couples whose estate value exceeds the $3.5 million tax exemption (or $7 million per couple) could help their heirs by purchasing life insurance to cover the estate taxes. This approach is especially beneficial if the inherited assets are illiquid—for example, a business or real estate property—and you want to ensure that your heirs will not have to sell the asset to pay the taxes. In the case of a couple, a "second-to-die" policy, which pays off after both insured parties have died, may be the most cost-efficient option. The second potential exception relates to the "pension maximization" concept introduced in Chapter 11. In this case, you would use life insurance to replace a spouse's pension or other retirement income that would terminate upon his or her death.

If you do determine that life insurance can play a valuable role in your estate plan, limit your options to permanent life insurance (as opposed to term insurance, which becomes prohibitively expensive as you get older) and highly rated insurance companies who will be around to honor their commitment.

Other Estate Planning Considerations to Handle Now

As scary as death seems to some people, a far more problematic issue that results from the great medical advances of the last century is that increasing numbers of people are living with severe mental or physical incapacities. To more fully protect yourself and your interests in the event of your own incapacity, make sure you include the following documents as part of your estate plan:

> ▷ **Durable Power of Attorney:** As people live longer there are more and more opportunities to suffer ailments like dementia and Alzheimer's disease that make it difficult or impossible for you to handle your financial affairs competently. A Durable Power of Attorney designates someone to act on your behalf when you're not able. Because of the far-reaching implications of this decision-making authority, you should name someone you trust implicitly and who understands and shares your interests. In most cases, the specified party is a family member but could also be a friend, attorney, accountant, or bank.

> ▷ **Health Care Proxy:** As we all saw during the national controversy regarding the removal of feeding tubes for Terri Schiavo, a young woman who had been in a vegetative state for 10 years, people have different beliefs and approaches to the use of life-sustaining treatment. A Heath Care Proxy can avoid this type of controversy by ensuring that *your* beliefs and desires are followed in the level of care you receive in a life-threatening medical situation. The Health Care Proxy designates one or more people to communicate your wishes.

> ▷ **Health Care Advance Directive:** Also known as a Do Not Resuscitate Order, a Health Care Advance Directive is a written order to medical caregivers not to attempt resuscitation in the event of cardiac or respiratory arrest. Depending on your state of residence, this form may have to be written by, signed by, or witnessed by a physician.

> ▷ **Living Will:** This statement represents the broadest perspective of your health-related wishes and may encompass aspects of both a Health Care Proxy and an Advance Directive.

As these are all legal documents, the specific requirements vary state by state, so it is imperative that you understand local requirements and, if you relocate, you revise the documents to abide by the new jurisdiction.

A Final Gift for Your Loved Ones

Although all of the documents discussed in this chapter are legal and official in nature, one of the most important documents you can leave for your survivors is an informal set of instructions. Whether in the form of a letter, a three-ring binder, or a manila folder with loose papers, this instruction set should provide an overview of your key financial and personal information and make the disposition of your estate go easier, faster, and less expensively for your heirs. The instruction set should include the following:

> ▷ Funeral arrangements, especially if you have made advance arrangements or have strong feelings regarding burial or cremation, regarding open or closed casket, or whether you would prefer to have donations made to a particular charity in lieu of flowers.

> ▷ A list of people who should be notified of your death.

> ▷ A list of key legal and financial advisors and institutions.

> ▷ A summary of your financial accounts and assets including insurance, pensions, brokerage accounts, mutual funds, bank accounts, and CDs.

> ▷ Information about any safe deposit boxes in your home or at a financial institution, along with the whereabouts of the key.

> ▷ A copy of your will—along with the location of the original.

> ▷ Your Social Security number and a copy of a recent Social Security payment or, if you haven't started collecting yet, a copy of your estimated benefits statement.

> ▷ Guidance regarding who among your survivors should receive family heirlooms and items of particular emotional value.

> ▷ Personal letters to your survivors.

These instructions should be reviewed and updated annually, and don't hide them where no one will ever find them. Your end-of-life instructions are only valuable if your estate executor and other loved ones know about their existence and where to find them. It's a simple way to remind everyone how much you loved them.

Chapter 15

I MPLEMENTED:
Putting it All Together

If you've begun reading this final chapter with the expectation that we will now reveal the secret sauce to a long and financially successful retirement, you're going to be disappointed. There is no magical formula or one-size-fits-all strategy for retirement. There are dozens, if not hundreds, of variables that affect each individual's strategy, tactics, and outcome. That means there is still work to be done, either on your own or with a financial advisor. This chapter provides a strong foundation, some fundamental beliefs and recommendations, and guidance on the kinds of questions and issues you need to answer and address.

Notwithstanding the uniqueness of each individual's retirement plan, everyone must recognize the three primary risk factors they'll face each and every year: market risk, inflation risk, and longevity risk. Each of these has been discussed elsewhere in the book, but their critical role in income-generation—and how their impact can be mitigated—mandates a quick review.

Market risk affects every investor at every stage of life. Fluctuations in the financial markets can send account balances soaring or sinking. And though market dips can be viewed as "buying opportunities" for the young who have many years to recoup their losses, retirees have neither the time nor the earning power to recover from deep losses. Accordingly, a retirement income plan requires strong defenses against market volatility. Your Nest Egg Game Plan can build those defenses with a higher allocation to fixed income and more exposure to diverse asset classes.

Inflation risk also affects all investors, but it represents the biggest danger to people living on fixed incomes. During one's working years, annual salary increases help keep pace with inflation. In retirement, other than Social Security and a small number of pension plans and annuities, you have to plan for and fight inflation on your own. To that end, your Nest Egg Game Plan portfolio should include an allocation to inflation-fighting asset classes like Treasury inflation-protected securities (TIPS), real estate, and commodities, using via low-cost ETFs or mutual funds.

Longevity risk, or the risk of outliving your assets, is the least understood and most frequently ignored aspect of retirement. It's also a problem that is going to get worse as healthcare improvements continue to extend human life. The sample scenarios put forth by Website calculators and simple financial planning tools often base their results on the average life expectancy (or roughly 85 years of age). Indeed, many of these computer simulations offer scientific-sounding conclusions such as, "at a 4.5% withdrawal rate you have a 90% chance of success through age 85." This type of pseudo-science nonsense serves to take your attention away from the 10-percent chance of failure and ignores creating a backup plan if you do end up in the 10-percent failure category. The only guaranteed solution to the longevity problem is an "annuitized" benefit (that is, a series of periodic payments, usually monthly, that will continue for life). Social Security and traditional defined benefit pension plans fall into the category. Fixed immediate annuities also offer a guaranteed solution to longevity risk and they should be included in most Nest Egg Game Plans. Indeed, as a general rule, we believe 25 to 75 percent of your retirement income needs should be achieved via annuitization.

After recognizing and understanding the risks you will face, it's time to develop your income generation plan. We'll guide you through this process by focusing on the five interlocking components that will drive your success:

> ▷ Strategies for creating income.

> ▷ An optimal portfolio structure.

> ▷ Annuitization for life and peace of mind.

> ▷ Diversification for the long haul.

> ▷ Monitoring and adjustment.

Strategies for Creating Income

The two overarching goals of your Nest Egg Game Plan are to maximize cash flow in retirement while maintaining sufficient assets to reduce or eliminate longevity risk. These goals are inherently at odds with each other, and the way you approach the conversion of assets into income will significantly impact whether the odds are in your favor or against you.

There are two ways to generate income from savings: annuitization and systematic withdrawals. The former will be considered in detail later in this chapter, so our focus here will be describing and comparing different approaches to systematic withdrawals. To wit:

> ▷ **Withdrawing interest and dividends only:** This is a time-honored approach that was embraced by our parents' and grandparents' generations. By never touching your principal, you're guaranteed never to run out of money but, unless your principal is in the millions of dollars, you're likely be forced to endure an unacceptable lifestyle.

ᐅ **Straight-line withdrawals:** This approach withdraws a fixed dollar amount (for example, $25,000), with or without cost-of-living adjustments (COLA), every year. Though this is exceptionally easy to understand and implement, this approach is basically a "dumbed-down" version of the next approach.

ᐅ **Fixed percentage of original portfolio value:** This approach is the most widely used and analyzed means of generating consistent retirement income and provides the basis for the illustrations we provide later in the chapter. In order to maintain one's lifestyle throughout retirement, this method should include annual cost-of-living adjustments (COLA) based on current inflation rates. The recommended fixed percentage withdrawal rate is in the 3-percent to 5-percent range.

ᐅ **Fixed percentage of year-end portfolio value:** This approach will almost certainly last a lifetime but is untenable for most people. The idea is that you withdraw the same percentage of each year's ending portfolio balance. Using 5 percent as an example and a portfolio value of $500,000, you would initially withdraw $25,000. The next year, if the portfolio was now worth $450,000, you would withdraw $22,500. Conversely, if the account was worth $550,000, you would withdraw $27,500. The drawback to this approach is your withdrawals are more likely to decrease over time rather than increase.

ᐅ **IRS required minimum distributions:** This method adapts the IRS rules for required minimum distributions from IRAs for use with one's overall investment portfolio. The benefit is that, by design, you will never run out of money. The drawback is that the withdrawal amounts will be quite low at younger ages and probably insufficient for most retirees.

This approach, however, is something you may want to transition into as you get older (perhaps beginning at ages 75 and up).

▷ **Variable withdrawal rates:** This approach provides the most flexibility but requires the closest monitoring. One method, which is too arcane to fully explain here, uses a rules-based formula to generate withdrawal rates that gradually increase as the retiree ages. Other methodologies require subjective decisions regarding when to increase or decrease withdrawals depending on market performance and spending needs. We believe that every approach to systematic withdrawal must include the flexibility to make mid-course adjustments and to evaluate the trade-offs that accompany every decision we make; however, a methodology that places no constraints or systematic ground rules on how much you can safely and appropriately withdraw offers far too many potential detours and dead-ends.

So what's the best approach for you? It depends. Our hope is that the information we've presented provides a solid foundation from which to make an informed determination of which approach is best for your circumstances. Most people, however, would be well served by using the fixed percentage of original portfolio value approach, adjusted annually for inflation, and that approach should be viewed as the default.

At the risk of contradicting ourselves and confusing our readers, we feel compelled to point out that every systematic withdrawal approach is fundamentally flawed and overly influenced by whatever point in time the withdrawals begin. Consider the case of two couples, Couple A and Couple B. Both have read this book, have built out their game plan, and are ready to go. They're both the same ages and they both have $1 million in retirement savings. The only difference is that Couple B retires exactly one year later than Couple A. So let's say Couple A retires on January 1, 2008. They settle on a 4-percent initial withdrawal rate and take monthly payments throughout the year totaling $40,000. The market swoon of 2008 affected both couples equally, with a loss of 20 percent. Couple B's portfolio is now worth $800,000 and Couple A's portfolio is worth slightly less: $760,000, due to the $40,000 in withdrawals. Couple B also settles on a 4-percent initial withdrawal rate, which will equal $32,000 in 2009. Couple A, however, will compute their 2009 withdrawal to equal $41,200—or the product of their initial withdrawal ($40,000) increased by a cost-of-living adjustment (assumed to be 3 percent).

It's difficult to justify why Couple A should be able to "safely" withdraw 29 percent more than Couple B, their virtually identical counterparts. We can't offer a solid explanation or defense of this disparity, other than to reiterate that flexibility is a critical component of every income-generation plan. Nothing that we or any other financial advisor, analyst, or media pundit says is carved in stone. Going back to our two-couple scenario, if Couple A truly lost 20% of their portfolio in one year, that would constitute a materially adverse event that would require a complete reformulation of their retirement game plan. Remaining rigidly committed to their initial formula accomplishes nothing but digging themselves deeper into a potentially bottomless pit.

An Optimal Portfolio Structure

Once you've determined your withdrawal strategy, you need to focus on the overall structure of your investment portfolio. Earlier in the book we discussed the relative merits of withdrawing money from taxable accounts before tapping your tax-deferred accounts, and we provided guidance on keeping tax-inefficient investments, like real estate and commodities, in tax-deferred accounts. As such, we're going to assume you've already considered those issues and have developed an optimal game plan. The next step is to identify and fund one or more "buckets" for your portfolio holdings. We strongly recommend a minimum of two buckets: an investment account and a cash account. We'll focus on this two-bucket approach but provide insight into alternative strategies as well.

Beginning at the moment of retirement, we believe everyone—*everyone*—should keep two years' worth of annual income needs in a totally liquid, 100-percent-safe cash account designed to cover their day-to-day living expenses. For the most part, this money should be invested in traditional bank savings accounts, short-term certificates of deposit, and money market accounts. Up to 10 percent of the cash account value could be invested in a high-quality, ultra-short-term bond mutual fund, but that approach should only be pursued if there is a meaningful difference in yield due to marketplace inefficiencies rather than safety issues. As part of the subprime mortgage debacle, some ultra-short-term bond funds from well-respected companies like Fidelity and Charles Schwab experienced double-digit losses in 2008.

This first bucket represents your "cash pantry" and constitutes a vital part of a well-diversified retirement income plan. Although it's exposed to inflation risk, this cash pantry is not susceptible to stock market volatility and, even more importantly, allows you to weather the effects of a bear market without having to sell beaten-down holdings to generate current income. In 2008 and early 2009, for example, the cash-pantry approach would have allowed you the luxury of not being forced to sell Apple, J.P. Morgan, or General Electric stock at ridiculously low prices only to see them double in value by May 2009. A cash pantry doesn't reduce market volatility, but rather it reduces the long- and short-term impact on your portfolio. Toward that end, as a general guideline, we recommend that you take your annual withdrawal from the investment account when the market is positive and withdraw from the cash account when market returns are negative. In addition, use the capital gain distributions, interest payments, and dividends from your investment account to maintain and replenish the cash account.

The second bucket is your investment account. This is where you're trying to deliver consistent returns and stay ahead of the inflationary bugaboo. If your initial withdrawal rate is 4 percent, approximately 92 percent of your portfolio will be in the investment account, with the other 8 percent in the cash account. We provide specific recommendations for allocating your investment account later in this chapter.

Some people like to further compartmentalize their investment portfolio, especially if they have multiple lifetime objectives. Psychological studies have learned that people like to segregate their money for specific uses. That's why, during working years, people often have specific savings designated in their mind as a college fund or vacation fund. For these people in particular, several investment pools may offer the optimal solution. For example, if you have a strong desire to leave an inheritance, you may want to create a legacy or charitable account. People who are very concerned about their healthcare needs may require a medical reserve fund (which could be funded with investment assets or take the form of a long-term care insurance policy).

As with all aspects of your Nest Egg Game Plan, flexibility is key. You may choose to start with just two buckets and then add others as your needs and desires change. Conversely, you may begin with multiple budgets and later determine that the extra effort is not warranted.

Annuitization for Life and Peace of Mind

Individuals readily insure themselves against a variety of risks during their working years. They buy life insurance as a hedge against the risk of premature death, as well as a host of other risk-management insurance products covering their health, homes, automobiles, boats, and other possessions. During retirement, the need for property and casualty insurance continues, but the need for life insurance (protecting against an early death) is replaced by the need for longevity insurance that "protects" us in case we live longer than we or the actuarial tables expect. This hedge can be delivered in the form of guaranteed lifetime fixed annuities. The questions are: How much of a hedge do you need, and what's the best way—economically and effectively—to acquire it?

The good news is most people begin retirement with some portion of their income already derived from annuity-like programs—Social Security and sometimes a company-provided pension plan. The bad news is twofold: Most folks don't understand the strategic benefits of lifetime fixed annuities, and they are reluctant to "lose control" of their money. The latter is the more interesting of the two issues and speaks volumes to the emotional aspects of money management. No one who receives a company pension ever complains about not having control over their money. Rather, they are delighted to receive their monthly check, and it never enters their mind that they could manage the money better and generate a higher return on their own. Oddly, however, when they receive a lump-sum payout from a 401(k) or profit-sharing plan, only a small minority of people choose to convert the money into the equivalent of a company pension plan by purchasing an immediate fixed annuity. There is something about having X amount of dollars in the bank that is theirs and that they can access anytime they want that pleases and comforts people. Unfortunately, what comforts people at age 65 may be the source of considerable unhappiness 20 or 30 years down the road. Nonetheless, you can't fight human nature, so we recommend a blend of "controlled" money and "annuitized" money.

Depending on your overall financial situation, and including Social Security and pension benefits, we recommend that a minimum of 25 percent of your retirement income needs be generated from annuitized money. The intent should be to generate a guaranteed monthly payment sufficient to meet your baseline living expenses (for example, rent or mortgage payments, food, utilities, and insurance premiums). The exception would be very wealthy individuals for whom longevity risk is non-existent. The less affluent you are, however, the higher percentage you may want to generate from annuitized money. Why? Because annuity product returns tend to be higher than what you could generate from traditional assets—which leads into a discussion of the strategic benefits of lifetime fixed annuities.

Let's begin with a look at actual annuity payout rates as of May 2009. All rates are based on a joint-life annuity covering a husband and wife of the same age. The annuities will pay the respective benefits for as long as either of the parties is alive. The income is not reduced when one of the parties dies and there are no payments to beneficiaries. Keep in mind, however, that these payments are not adjusted for inflation (although some fixed annuity products do offer that benefit for an additional cost). Payout rates for individuals, as opposed to couples, would be substantially higher.

Joint Life Annuity With $100,000 Deposit

	65	70	75	80	85
Monthly Income	$575	$645	$729	$852	$1,032
Annual Income	$6,900	$7,740	$8,748	$10,224	$12,384
"Withdrawal" Percentage	6.9%	7.4%	8.7%	10.2%	12.4%

As you can see from the table, the older you are the higher income stream you can generate, but, even at age 65, the initial withdrawal rate is a hefty 6.9 percent. If you allocated 25 percent of your portfolio to a fixed annuity and utilized a 4-percent initial withdrawal rate for the rest of your retirement Nest Egg, you could generate a blended withdrawal rate of 4.72 percent. A 50-percent allocation to a fixed annuity at age 65 would deliver a 5.45-percent blended initial withdrawal rate.

The table includes a range of starting ages because we strongly recommend a "laddered" approach, similar to what you would do with individual bonds, when investing in fixed annuities. Like bonds, fixed annuities are highly affected by prevailing interest rates. The higher the interest rate at the time of purchase, the higher your lifetime payout. The preceding table represents payout rates in May 2009 when interest rates were at an all-time low (the federal funds rate had a target of 0.0 percent to 0.25 percent). The same table, using payout rates from the early 1980s, would include monthly income rates at least 50-percent higher than the ones we've illustrated. Once you've determined your target allocation to fixed immediate annuities, spread out your investments over five to 10 years gaining exposure to a variety of interest rate environments.

You should also give serious consideration to a "longevity annuity" or deferred-income annuity. This strategy provides an effective way to boost your withdrawal rate in the early years of retirement without worrying about running out of money later in life. Here's how it works. At age 65 you purchase a longevity annuity with a lump-sum payment, and then forget about it for the next 20 years. At age 85 you start receiving a monthly payment that will last for the rest of your life. The downside is that if you die before age 85, you lose it all and your beneficiaries receive nothing. That's why this strategy is only appropriate for a small portion of your overall portfolio. The upside, however, is dramatic because, like life insurance, this is a pure hedge whose value is leveraged upward because your money is pooled with thousands of other people. As an example, for $71,000 a 65-year-old male can purchase a longevity annuity that will pay $60,000 a year beginning at age 85. That kind of guaranteed benefit can provide substantial peace of mind and, we believe, is appropriate for many if not most retirees. If you decide that a longevity annuity is right for you, purchase it as soon as you retire. The longer you wait to buy a longevity annuity, the more it will cost for the same level of benefits.

One final point. The guarantees offered by fixed annuities are backed by the financial strength of the issuing company. As with all products, some companies are stronger than others. Do some comparison shopping as rates vary from company to company, but limit your comparisons to highly rated insurance companies with long track records and sterling reputations.

Diversification for the Long Haul

The recommended investment portfolio for retirees used to consist of nothing but investment-grade U.S. bonds and certificates of deposit. In recent years, partly in response to increased longevity and partly due to the seemingly low-risk "easy money" that was being made in the stock market of the 1980s and 1990s, financial professionals started advocating larger and larger allocations to stocks. The reasoning was that your retirement might last as long as your working days and you needed the extra return that stocks can deliver. Now we're seeing a resurgence of the traditional belief that the percentage of your portfolio represented by bonds should equal your age, although some particularly risk-averse investors are jumping back on the 100-percent fixed-income bandwagon.

Our approach is slightly different and more representative of real-life needs and risk tolerances. The investment portfolio we recommend is specifically designed to complement the annuitization strategy and cash-pantry concept we introduced earlier. That means you have already funded a guaranteed fixed income stream and you have put aside two years' worth of income needs into a liquid cash account.

The next step is to establish a multi-asset balanced portfolio consisting of stocks, bonds, cash, and diversifying assets. The basic asset allocation should follow a 40/60 rule, with 40 percent of the portfolio invested in equity and equity-like assets (stocks, real estate, and commodities) and 60 percent in bonds and cash. (Note that the cash allocation is *in addition* to the two years' worth of income needs deposited in your cash pantry.)

Asset Allocation for Multi-Asset Balanced Portfolio
(not including 2 years' of withdrawals
in cash account)

Large U.S.	Small U.S.	Non-U.S.	U.S. Bonds	Cash	REIT	Commodities
8%	8%	8%	50%	10%	8%	8%

Though still exposed to stock and bond market volatility, the broad diversification we suggest minimizes the dramatic ups and downs and has a built-in inflationary hedge via the real estate and commodities exposure. If there were a secret sauce it would be the low correlation between the seven asset classes. You'll recall from Chapter 11 that, from an investing standpoint, correlation refers to the relative price movement of two asset classes. Correlation values range from +1.00 to -1.00. If two assets have a correlation close to +1.00 they tend to perform very similarly (in other words, they go up and down at the same time and at similar speeds). If two assets have a correlation close to -1.00 they are said to be inversely correlated. That means when one goes up in value the other goes down, and vice versa. A low correlation value approaching zero (0.00) indicates that the two assets move totally independent of each other. When building an investment portfolio you want to minimize the number of high correlations (above 0.70) between the various asset classes. As you can see in the accompanying table, the diversification of our Multi-Asset Balanced Portfolio offers impressively low correlations. Of the 21 correlations among the asset classes, only four are above the 0.70 level and one-third are at or below the 0.14 level.

Multi-Asset Balanced Portfolio
10-Year Correlations of
Monthly Returns
January 1999–December 2008

	Small U.S.	Non-U.S.	Real Estate	Commodities	U.S. Bonds	Cash
Large U.S.	0.72	0.80	0.74	0.27	0.21	0.05
Small U.S.		0.78	0.69	0.35	0.21	0.03
Non-U.S.			0.66	0.43	0.23	(0.08)
Real Estate				0.34	0.48	0.02
Commodities					0.14	0.02
U.S. Bonds						0.07

The benefit derived from this highly non-correlated portfolio is twofold: less volatility and higher returns. Let's take a look.

This first chart shows how a $500,000 starting balance (with $459,328 in the investment account and $40,672 in the cash-pantry account) would have performed from 1970 through 2008. The assumptions are a 4-percent initial withdrawal rate increased annually with a 4-percent cost-of-living adjustment. After 39 years, the portfolio provided a total of $1.8 million in withdrawals and the remaining balance equals $6.6 million plus $181,000 in the cash account.

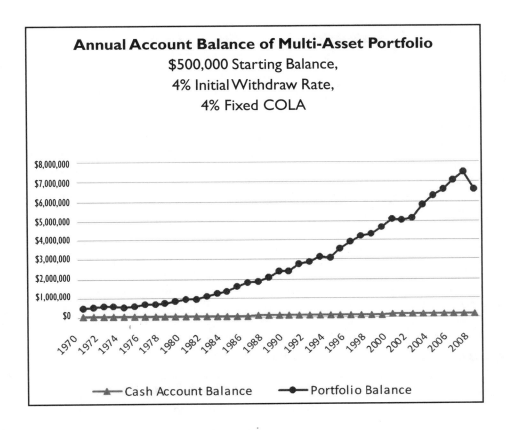

Annual Account Balance of Multi-Asset Portfolio
$500,000 Starting Balance,
4% Initial Withdraw Rate,
4% Fixed COLA

Now as a point of comparison, we're repeating a chart from Chapter 3. This example shown on page 236 represents a plain vanilla portfolio split—50 percent in U.S. stocks and 50 percent in U.S. bonds. The withdrawal and inflation assumptions are the same as with the multi-asset portfolio. This strategy also worked well, though not quite as well as its multi-asset counterpart. The ending balance is $5 million, and the 39-year ride was much bumpier than the smooth trajectory of the multi-asset portfolio.

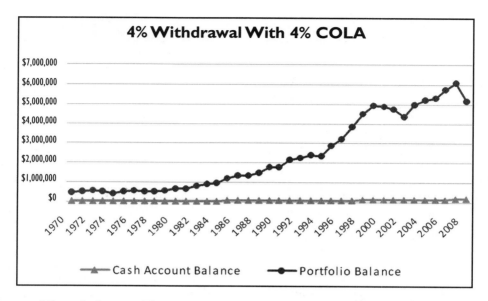

Now, let's consider a more demanding scenario in which the annual cost-of-living adjustment equals the consumer price index, rather than a fixed 4-percent annual increase.

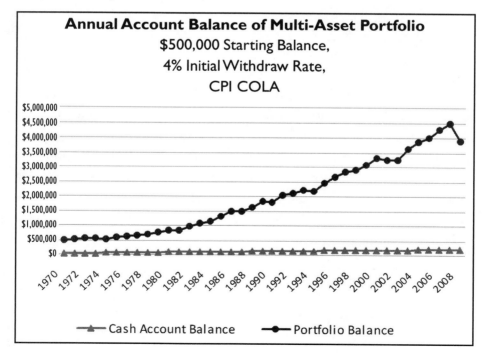

As you can see, the real-life cost-of-living adjustments caused the ending account balance of the multi-asset portfolio to decline by more than $2.5 million. Nonetheless, the portfolio withstood the more demanding cost-of-living adjustments based on the actual Consumer Price Index.

In addition to the cost-of-living adjustment, another key variable in the "survivability" of a retirement income portfolio is the initial withdrawal rate. Thus far we've been using 4 percent, which, based on a portfolio with a starting balance of $500,000, delivers $20,000 of income in the first year. Now, let's see what happens when the initial withdrawal rate moves to 5 percent, or $25,000. We will maintain the CPI-based COLA and, as shown in the following chart, the impact is dramatic. Instead of an ending portfolio balance of nearly $4 million, we now end the 39-year period with a balance of about $680,000, combined with a cash account balance in excess of $200,000.

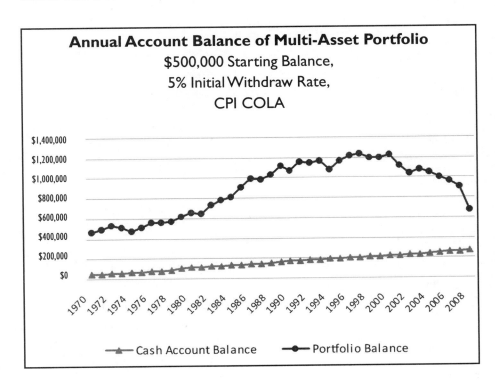

Increasing from 5 percent to a withdrawal rate of 6 percent causes the portfolio to fail after 24 years with the cash account sustaining the retiree for an additional two years. (Rather than repeating another chart from Chapter 3, look back on your own and see that, based on the same assumptions, the multi-asset portfolio endured for six years longer than the 50-percent stock and 50-percent bond portfolio.) Much of this scenario's demise can be attributed to the high inflation levels of the late 1970s and early 1980s, which, when mixed with the high initial withdrawal rate, created a toxic combination.

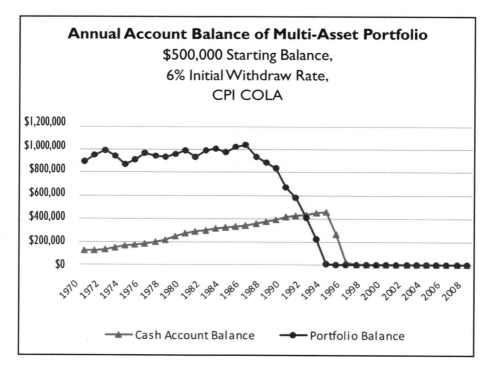

Although it would be difficult to recommend a 6-percent withdrawal rate based on this data, the scenario does offer a case in point where a longevity annuity purchased at age 65 (in 1970) with payments beginning at age 85 (in 1990) when the account value was more than $300,000 could have turned a failed plan into a successful one.

The next scenario reflects the three stages of retirement we introduced back in Chapter 1. During the first stage of retirement, people tend to be more active and spend money on travel and other forms of recreation. During the middle stage, retirees often slow down and spend more leisure time at home with friends and family. As a result, their spending levels and income needs tend to decrease. The third stage often entails increased healthcare expenditures and costs go up. If that's the reality for most people, then why are retirement income simulations always based on a static withdrawal rate? That's a rhetorical question because we know the answer: A static withdrawal rate is easier to program and illustrate. We learned that ourselves in creating the graphic following on page 240, but the story it tells more than justifies the effort. In this "Phased Approach" to retirement income we again use the multi-asset portfolio, and we begin with an initial withdraw rate of 6 percent, which we'll use for the first 10 years. The next 10 years (approximately associated with 75 to 85-year-olds) utilizes a withdrawal rate of 4 percent to account for the reduced spending levels associated with less active pursuits. Finally, the withdrawal rate increases to 5 percent and remains there for the final 19 years to account for increased health expenditures.

Under this phased withdrawal rate approach, the portfolio remains durable for the full 39 years, ending with a balance of about $95,000 and a cash account balance of nearly $270,000. Take a moment to compare this graphic with the earlier chart that illustrated an initial withdrawal rate of 6 percent that remained static, except for inflationary adjustments. You'll see that the first 10 years track identically, but then the illustrations diverge dramatically. The static 6-percent scenario reaches a peak value of about $525,000 and then begins a free-fall in 1986, whereas the 6-percent–4-percent–5-percent scenario peaks at $1 million and endures for the entire period.

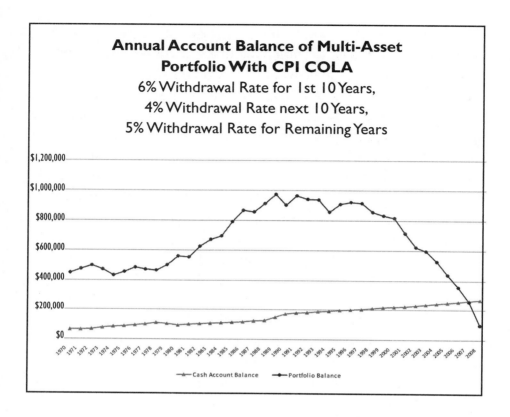

All of the examples in this section spring from the Multi-Asset Balanced Portfolio consisting of large U.S. stocks, small U.S. stocks, foreign stocks, U.S. bonds, cash, real estate, and commodities. We have purposely limited the number of asset classes discussed in order to keep the information simple and to reduce the transaction costs, tax implications, and complexities required to manage and rebalance a more diverse portfolio. Moreover, we have performance data starting in 1970 for the seven core assets that comprise the Multi-Asset Balanced Portfolio.

Investors who are willing to invest considerable time and attention to their portfolio should consider the following asset allocation model known as the "7Twelve Portfolio" shown on page 241. We believe this portfolio offers the optimum balance of risk and reward. It follows the same 40-60 formula used by the Multi-Asset Balanced Portfolio, with 40 percent allocated to equities and equity-like investments and 60 percent in fixed income investments; however, the allocations are further refined to include sub-asset classes like emerging markets, international bonds, and Treasury inflation-protected securities. Since 1998 (which is as far back as we can get performance history for all 12 of the asset classes), this asset allocation model has delivered strong returns with moderate volatility, and, although past performance is no guarantee of future results, the breadth of asset classes in the model should continue to work well in any economic environment.

Approximately 40% of the Portfolio Allocation in Equity and Diversifying Assets				Approximately 60% of the Portfolio Allocation in Bonds and Cash		
U.S. Equity	Non-U.S. Equity	Real Estate	Resources	U.S. Bonds	Non-U.S. Bonds	Cash
5% Large Companies	5% Developed Markets	5% Global Real Estate	5% Natural Resources	30% Aggregate Bonds	10% International Bonds	10% U.S. Money Market
5% Medium-sized Companies	5% Emerging Markets		5% Commodities	10% Inflation Protected Bonds (TIPS)		
5% Small Companies						

As we have stressed throughout the book, inexpensive index funds and exchange traded funds offer the most appropriate vehicles to build your multi-asset retirement portfolio. More detailed information about multi-asset portfolios can be obtained at Craig's Website (*www.7TwelvePortfolio.com*).

As strongly as we believe that we've presented a portfolio that can deliver the optimum balance between risk and reward, we must remind you that every individual's situation is different. Different levels of wealth and different temperaments require decidedly different approaches. Despite what you read in the press, there is no law that says every 75-year-old must have exposure to the stock market. Some individuals may be best served by a portfolio composed solely of FDIC-insured and investment-grade fixed-income products. Others may prefer the absolute security achieved by annuitizing 100 percent of their portfolio. Always remember that this is money you earned, and you have the inalienable right to determine how it will be invested.

Monitoring and Adjustment

Generating lifetime income is a lifetime job. Thinking you can "set it and forget it" will ultimately result in an imbalanced and inefficient portfolio unable to support your goals and desires. (Refer back to the Couple A and Couple B scenario if you have any doubts about that statement.) An effective retirement income strategy requires ongoing monitoring and review. If you work with a financial advisor, he or she should conduct an annual review. If you choose to do this on your own, you still need to review your results and progress against your long-term plan. Reviewing your portfolio is especially critical during the early years of retirement when your spending is more likely to exceed your targeted withdrawal rate.

A critical part of the review process is identifying and quantifying the effects of major life events. The death of a spouse, illness, relocation, and similar life events all have a major impact on your retirement plan. Sometimes the impact is so significant that you may need to start over and build your retirement income plan from scratch (albeit with a little more experience under your belt).

Sometimes you'll need to adjust your plan because of external factors like market performance, interest rates, or inflationary pressures. Oftentimes people assume that mid-course adjustments are always negative in nature, but the opposite can also be true. It's not uncommon for individuals to begin their retirement with overly conservative assumptions and strategies. After several years—and several annual reviews to assess progress against plan—they may find they are unnecessarily constraining their spending and feel comfortable loosening their portfolio's purse strings a bit. Your Nest Egg Game Plan is a living entity that requires care and tending to reach its full potential. It takes time and effort, but the payback is truly priceless.

Some Final Thoughts

We've been writing this book during the worst global economic crisis since the Great Depression. Our Nest Eggs, like most of yours, are looking quite a bit more fragile than they did in the autumn of 2007. We're not kicking ourselves, however, about what we should have done and how we should have seen it coming. We're also not doubling-down to try to earn back our losses as quickly as as possible. We still believe strongly in the benefits of asset allocation and the true diversification achieved from non-correlating asset classes. We still believe in a systematic approach to investing that relegates emotion to the sidelines. And we believe deeply that the United States and the American people will emerge from this crisis stronger and more committed to our democratic principles and entrepreneurial philosophies than ever before. We'll probably also be a little smarter and a little less driven by greed and avarice. Instead of living beyond our means and wanting what we don't have, we'll better appreciate all the privileges, freedoms, and comforts we already possess.

In a very real sense, the "Great Recession" of 2008 provides an opportunity for the country and each of us to begin again, to rethink our priorities, and to truly reinvent ourselves. This idea of a fresh start is also a great way to think about retirement. In retirement, the future is yours to do with as you please. Our goal has been to provide the financial foundation that will allow you to maximize your potential in retirement. The rest is up to you.

As we said way back in the Introductory chapter,

"This is your money and your life;

enjoy every penny and

every second of it."

I NDEX

ABOUT THE AUTHORS

PHIL FRAGASSO

Phil Fragasso has more than 20 years of experience in financial services. He is currently president of I-Pension LLC, a registered investment advisory firm. Prior to his current position he held executive-level positions at Rydex Investments, Columbia Funds, and Sun Life Financial.

Phil's diverse experience has one common element: a focus on translating arcane and complicated subject matter into language that is simple and understandable. Whether discussing investment strategies, mutual funds, ETFs, or asset allocation theories, Phil puts himself in the place of the end-customer and crafts messages that resonate and motivate. As an investment advisor working with clients, Phil believes he has an obligation to educate and explain the full array of investment options available before recommending a particular solution. And through all interactions with his clients, Phil stresses that "it's your money." His role is to advise and guide, serve as a sounding board, and remove some of the emotion that often clouds people's investment decisions.

Phil's drive and passion have built a reputation for innovative thinking and creative leadership. He has been a guest lecturer at Babson College and Emerson College, and has been a frequent speaker at financial services industry conferences. His presentation skills consistently receive high marks, and he regularly speaks to the press on behalf of his firm.

With a wife, two children, and two yellow Labrador retrievers, Phil leads an active and balanced life. Writing has always been a key driver of his personal satisfaction, and *The Nest Egg Pension Plan* is the latest entry in a growing list of published works.

CRAIG L. ISRAELSEN

Craig L. Israelsen, PhD, is an associate professor at Brigham Young University (Provo, Utah), where he teaches Personal and Family Finance to more than 1,200 students each year. He holds a PhD in family resource management from Brigham Young University. He received a BS in agribusiness and an MS in agricultural economics from Utah State University. Prior to teaching at BYU, he was on the faculty of the University of Missouri-Columbia for 14 years, where he taught Personal and Family Finance.

Primary among Craig's research interests is the analysis of mutual funds and the design of investment portfolios. He writes monthly for *Financial Planning* magazine, and is a regular contributor to the *Journal of Indexes* and *Horsesmouth.com.* His research has also been published in the *Journal of Financial Planning, Journal of Asset Management (U.K.), Journal of Performance Measurement, Asia Financial Planning Journal (Singapore), Journal of Family and Economic Issues,* and *Financial Counseling and Planning.*

Craig's research has been cited in the *Christian Science Monitor, Wall Street Journal, Newsweek, Forbes, Smart Money* magazine, *Kiplinger Retirement Report, Advisor Perspectives, Dow Jones Market Watch, Family Circle,* and *Bottom Line Personal.*

He is a principal at Target Date Analytics, LLC (*www.TDBench.com*), a firm that has developed indexes for the benchmarking and evaluation of target date/lifecycle funds.

Craig is married to Tamara Trimble. They have seven children (Sara, Andrew, Heidi, Mark, Nathan, Emma, and Jared). Hobbies include running, biking, swimming, woodworking, and family vacations. He has competed in the Boston Marathon five times, but has never won.